You're Full of Shift

You're Full of Shift

101 Stories of Shift

HOWARD MILLER

Fulcrum Point
San Francisco

You're Full of Shift
Published in the United States by
Fulcrum Point
30 Crestline Drive, Suite 2
San Francisco CA 94131
415-642-0843
www.fulcrumpointpartners.com

Second edition published 2009.

ISBN: 978-0-984-39950-5

Printed in the United States of America

This book is dedicated to my father, George Miller, who in one moment taught me that something which may seem difficult at first can shift to a moment of wonder and opportunity.

I'd like to thank the following people, who in one way or another, or in multiple ways, helped me to develop this book. Some of you helped in obvious ways; some of you really don't know how your words inspired me!

My sincere thanks to: Lila Miller, Andy Miller, Stuart McFaul, Paolo Miranda, John Harrison, Nannette Carroll, Zander Sprague, Beth Proudfoot, Edith Yeung, Michael Lee, Beth Miller, Trudy Triner, Eric Ball, Kristi Matal, Tom Pelliccioni and Karen Gee.

Thank you for your assistance, enthusiasm, support and encouragement!

How this Book Came To Be

Truth be told, I didn't intend to write a book, and I didn't know as I wrote some of these things which happened they would be part of this collection of stories.

When I started my business I needed a way to communicate with my clients. So I began writing stories about incidents which happened in my daily life. I didn't call these incidents difficult situations, but there was always an "a-ha" moment in each of them.

I named these stories "soundbites" and started emailing them to my clients every two to three weeks

My readers commented on how much they enjoyed the stories and encouraged me to put them in a book. These comments kept coming. My readership kept at a constant level (and still does).

Developing the theme of the book was initially a struggle.

At first I thought all of the stories were about stress. I started to relate the stories to the five stages of stress, similar to the five stages of dying: fighting stress, fearing stress, learning from stress, accepting stress, and embracing stress.

But this didn't ring true to me.

Finally I realized all of the stories revolved around conflict-- conflict with others or conflict with myself.

Initially I wanted to match each story to a specific step in my three step process which I created and is described in the introduction. This didn't work as each story really contains all three steps.

Then there was the question of order.

I happened to be reading a book by Bill Maher at the time. He arranged his articles in alphabetical order. It seemed so simple.

A light went off for me – I'll put my stories in alphabetical order!

Now, looking back, the journey seems to have come to an obvious conclusion, but it didn't seem this way as I was figuring everything out.

How comforting to watch this process unfold in such a great way and to know that these stories, which seem so subtle and inconsequential at first, can produce an entirely different outcome if we only shift our thoughts and actions.

Howard Miller

Introduction

A few years ago I was visiting my parents. I get along very well with my folks but there are certain topics I try to stay clear of with my dad. Specifically the topic of the Middle East.

You see, we disagree on what needs to be done there. Actually I don't know if this is true. We never get that far in our conversations.

What really happens is we both say things which contradict each other. The conversation gets tense and heated. We both start to get angry. Then one of us gets angrier than the other one. Pretty soon we are yelling and screaming at each other. But, what we're yelling and screaming about has nothing to do with the Middle East, but about what happened in 1972 when I was a teenager.

So I created a rule for myself: don't bring up these topics with my dad.

During this particular visit I forgot my rule and started to have one of those conversations. As the tension got more and more heated, I kept thinking to myself, *I'm not going to get angry. I'm not going to get angry.*

I was already angry.

Then my dad looked at me, sighed and said, *"Where did I go wrong?"*

In the past this would have been the send off moment, the moment where the window was busted and all bets were off.

I would have started with something like: *What do you mean where did I go wrong? How dare you? I'm a great son. How can you question that? What kind of monster are you? What father questions their son this way?*

But this time I didn't do this.

Instead I paused, took a breath, looked at my dad and said, *"Gee Dad, I don't know where you went wrong. I'm going for a walk. Do you want to worry about it or join me?"*

He laughed. I laughed. And, in that single moment, we obliterated more than 30 years of behavior.

This unassuming and subtle moment (which by the way my dad doesn't even remember) changed our relationship. We are closer then we have ever been.

As a result, my trust in others has grown, thereby increasing my confidence and energy. My business life has also flourished due to this increased energy.

I was astonished by this change and wondered how it happened.

I had no idea.

A miracle had occurred, but I couldn't grasp what exactly happened.

So over the last several years, I have made it my business to examine other moments in my life as well as those of my clients to find out what happens when a difficult situation with a difficult person can shift to a positive opportunity.

My observations led me to three different strategies you can use to shift a difficult situation to a positive opportunity:

- Be <u>aware</u> of the situation and attempt to look at it differently.
- Take <u>ownership</u>, recognizing how you are contributing to the situation.
- Take <u>action</u> to change the situation.

If you are able to do any one—or all three—of these things, a shift could happen.

The capacity for each of us to experience shifts is limitless. Any moment can be an opportunity to see things differently, to transform something viewed as negative into something positive.

If we took this opportunity once a day, one moment a day, what could the potential be? How could this affect our relationships, our wealth, and our outlook on life?

One moment, not planned between my dad and me, transformed my life. What if I <u>consciously</u> use the process I used <u>unconsciously?</u> How might it transform my life?

This book looks at other moments in my life where I made a transformation by *resetting my expectations, re-examining my beliefs,* or *changing the pace at which I reacted.*

We have limitless shifts within us.

We are all full of shift.

Here are some of my stories of shift.

May they help you remember situations in your life where you had a shift. More importantly, may they inspire you to be more conscious of the power you have to make shifts in the future.

Stories of Shift

$9.92

I had an emergency root canal. After insurance, the bill was over $1000.

I received a couple of invoices for the amount I owed. I called the dental office and told them when I would pay the bill. I paid it when I told them I would.

Imagine my reaction when I got a follow-up bill for the amount I had not paid: $9.92. This was the interest applied for the extra time it had taken me to pay the bill.

I was furious.

I called the office and demanded they remove the charge. The administrator at the other end refused, saying it wouldn't be fair to the other patients. I argued to no avail.

My patience was thin. The office manager was on vacation and I requested (okay demanded) she call me when she returned.

I felt ripped off and wronged. I was prepared to fight to the end even though I knew no collection agency would take over a collection of such a low amount.

I felt I was fighting the cause for "Everyman", the battle against those businesses which charge outrageous fees and rip us off.

I was on fire. It wasn't about the money, it was the cause.

Suddenly, I remembered I was fighting about $9.92.

I also considered the *real cause and what I really wanted.*

I felt foolish.

The truth was while I didn't want to pay the small amount, it wasn't me vs. them. I had made it this way and had gotten what I had asked for: A fight!

I realized it wasn't worth my time or energy.

I didn't really have to pay the money. Sure, if by some remote chance it would affect my credit rating, I would pay.

I released the incident and the energy I was giving it.

The following week the office manager called me. I had forgotten about the matter, so her call took me by surprise.

I explained to her that I understood why there was a small finance charge, but I wanted it removed as an act of courtesy.

So she did.

When I was prepared for a fight I got a fight. When I let go, I ended up getting what I really wanted.

Once again I realized:

- What I focus on is what I get
- If I think the proverbial "they" are out to get me, then "they" will be out to get me no matter what "they" say or do.
- It's so much nicer to be nice!

A fight is so much easier to win when you don't have it.

A Little More Effort

My workout partner and I were at the gym, preparing to do our chest routine. We needed to wait for another patron to finish using the bench press. When the guy finished we told him to leave the weights, and we'd take care of putting them away.

He had been lifting 45 pound weights.. We decided to start with those although we normally we work up to 45 pounds by our 3rd or 4th set. But we were both feeling pretty lazy and didn't want to move the 45 pounders off the bar and put on 35's.

Because we started with 45's we ended up lifting higher than we normally do. Higher than what I've lifted in several years.

In addition, we worked out harder during the rest of the workout.

I had no expectations of working harder. In fact I was feeling low energy and could have coasted through our workout.

But it didn't take much effort to lift the extra weight, and as a result, I felt more energized when we were done.

How often do I coast through things instead of giving a little more effort?

When I give *anything* a little more effort:

- I get better results
- I am living larger
- I am happier about everything

By my fourth set I was lifting 20 pounds over what I typically lift. I didn't complete many repetitions (okay, three), but that's three more than I thought possible.

I will do it again.

Soon.

Next week.

I don't know when.

I'll do it when I remember that it only takes *a little more effort.*

Accepting Compliments

My phone rang one evening just as I was getting home. It was three friends I hadn't seen in awhile. They were hanging out together and had gotten to reminiscing about good times they had shared in the past. My name came to mind, and they promptly called me to tell me.

Okay, they were drunk.

But, it was uplifting to get such a compliment.

I could have brushed it off because they were drinking. I could have put it aside because it wasn't part of what I was doing at the time, and it wasn't on my mind.

But, it made me stop and be appreciative.

It took me out of my ordinary moment and made that moment special.

By being open to the compliment:

- I accepted the value I have on others
- I could appreciate how the past can show up in memorable ways in the present
- I felt special

When someone gives me a compliment, if I think the compliment is not true, and I feel embarrassed, I am doing that person a disservice by not accepting a wonderful gift.

If I have trouble accepting a compliment, the solution is rather easy. I only need to say two words:

Thank you!

Accepting Gifts

I was out with some friends, and one of them offered to buy me a pair of jeans. I immediately refused the offer. Actually I got defensive, indignant, and a little angry. I could buy my own jeans. I don't need a friend to offer me such an extravagance. Offer me a coffee or a drink, but not a pair of jeans.

I argued strongly in not accepting the gift. The generous offer didn't seem right to receive. My friend looked at me and said, "If you can't learn to accept gifts from people who care about you, how can you expect all the love you want and deserve in your life to show up?"

This comment made me pause to consider his generous offer and my steadfast and immediate refusal. I realized I hadn't asked for this gift; it was being offered. A gift of a pair of jeans, really a gift of love and friendship, from someone I care about and who cares about me.

In a brief moment I changed my mind and accepted his offer.

I then asked for matching shirts to go with the jeans.

My friend said no.

But when I opened up to this gift of love it made me really present to the moment and made it more realistic for people to accept my gifts to them. If I don't accept gifts from others, why should they accept gifts from me?

This experience made me wonder:

- What would my life be like if I were more open to accepting what is in front of me?
- Who would be in my life if I were more accepting of gifts?
- In my life right now, whose gifts am I not accepting?

So, if any of you have gifts to offer, I'll gladly accept them.

Howard Miller

All I Have on Me Are My Gloves and iPod

Arriving at the gym for my workout, I realized I had forgotten my lock for the locker. Not a big deal, I thought and took what I needed , leaving the rest of my things in my car.

Toward the end of my work out I wondered, *where are my car keys?* They weren't in my pocket.

I figured I had left them by the treadmill.

They weren't there.

Wait, they were most likely in the stretching room. They must have fallen out of my pocket when I was stretching..

They weren't there.

I went to the front desk to see if anyone had found a set of keys.

No.

I retraced all my steps.

I couldn't find the keys.

I didn't want to believe I had locked the keys in the trunk of my car. It would have been stupid and almost impossible to do – I would have had to open up the trunk, intentionally put my key into my gym bag, place the bag back in the trunk, and close the trunk.

After I retraced my steps several times, I asked a few people if they had seen any keys. No one had found them, so I needed to accept that they were missing.

There I was, sweating after working out, with only my workout gloves and iPod shuffle and with no way to get into my car or my house and with no money. And, I had to be at an out-of-town work appointment in about two hours.

The guy at the front desk showed me a phone I could use.

Since my cell phone was also in my car there were only two people I could call. Who remembers phone numbers these days?

One friend lived nearby and might be around at this time of day. I decided to try him. As I called him, I realized he may not answer the phone because he wouldn't recognize the number from which I was calling.

He didn't answer the phone.

After leaving him a message and trying him about five more times, I finally got an answer. We talked out options, and I decided it would be easier and less costly, although possibly more time consuming, to try to get into my apartment rather then break into my car. I was optimistic a friend who lived nearby and had my keys might be working from home – he often did so on Fridays (although I had no idea if today would be an exception). Or, my landlord might be home and could let me in.

My friend agreed to come and meet me at the gym. Fortunately, the weather was nice, so hanging around outside was pleasant.

I decided to check my car for the keys one more time when the guy who worked at the front desk came running out – with a set of keys! A member of the cleaning staff had found them!

I called my friend and told him not to come by!

On my way home, I was energized and relieved. I realized as I was driving:

- Because I was temporarily unable to get into my own space (my car and home), I felt a great sense of gratitude when I was able to return to them.

- By not panicking, and instead reaching out for help, I was able to assume an attitude of acceptance.
- Having a friend who was able to be there for me in an emergency left me feeling humbled and loved.

And I'm sure glad I hadn't locked my keys in the car!

All My Children

I admit it. I watched *All My Children* from 1981 to the beginning of 2005.

I watched this show for 24 years. *And* it is one of the longest relationships I've had with anything.

I didn't watch everyday for 24 years. I recall a six month gap where I didn't watch (When I stopped watching, Tad was being chased by his psychotic twin Ted and was left hanging on a cliff, and when I resumed watching Tad was re-marrying Dixie for the third time.

But other than that brief hiatus, through a cross-country move and changes of careers, relationships, and friends, *All My Children* was a constant. Why?

I used to say I watched it for three reasons:

1. As a performer, I enjoyed watching actors on the show become better or worse at their craft during their duration on the show
2. I liked the absurdity of the situations. One day could take three months to unfold, yet a five year old could grow to the age of 19 in two years!
3. Susan Lucci as Erica Kane.

Then one day, after 24 years, I wondered why I was still watching the show.
The reasons I had given for watching no longer applied. I can observe actors on other shows, the absurd situations didn't amuse me anymore, and Susan (bless her heart) has done everything she possibly could with her character.

I realized I was watching out of habit, I had gone completely unconscious, most likely several years prior.

So I stopped watching.

Immediately.

I didn't miss it. I still don't watch. I doubt I ever will.

I don't judge myself for watching all those years. I don't beat myself up for letting something get to be a habit without providing any benefits.

I can't tell you what I've done with the time saved by no longer watching (no, I don't watch another soap opera!).

I do realize part of me watched because I wanted to obtain something which never can be guaranteed in real life—a sense of certainty, a sense of knowing what is going to happened to me.

On the soap opera, each character is given a plot line. What will happen to each character is pre-determined.

A part of me would like to know what will happen to me! Wouldn't it be nice to know what will happen in the next few months to my business, my love life, and my friends?

But if I did know, then what? What would I do? I'd be going through the motions of life because I already knew what was going to happen.

In every moment, I can choose what to do. Even if life were "pre-destined," I can still live each moment to its fullest.

When I realize I can make *each* moment count:

- I give each moment more of my all
- I stay more conscious with what I'm doing
- I get more real with what I'm doing, and can avoid doing things merely out of habit.

Escape can be great! Wanting to get away from it all is human and can be relaxing and thought provoking.

Doing the same thing for too long without thinking about it doesn't work for me.

All the Work I Did Is Gone!

I had gathered information for a project. My research involved making phone calls and documenting everything in a spreadsheet. All told, I had completed many hours of work.

A couple of days later, I went to work on the spreadsheet and couldn't find it. I didn't panic because I was on my laptop and had created the original document on my desktop. I obviously didn't transfer the file to my flash drive. I was a little disappointed that I couldn't work on it right then but figured I could do it later in the day.

When I got home, I couldn't find the document on my desktop either.

Not in any folder.

Not in the recycle bin.

That's when I panicked.

While in my panic state, I wondered how this could happen.

I'm not sure why I spent the energy wondering how it happened because it wouldn't make the document magically appear.

I ended up recreating the spreadsheet. It took some time but not really as long as the original investment of time.

When I panicked, I felt hopeless. I had lost control and couldn't retrieve the work I had already done.

But why feel hopeless?

I was able to recreate the document. It was a tedious task, but it got done.

I saw a movie back in the 80's called *Hope and Glory*. In the movie, the family's house caught on fire. The boy was crying, and the mother comforted him by telling him it was only things which were destroyed. *They* were okay.

Isn't this the truth?

I recreated what I had done. It may not have been the exact duplication, but the original was a work in progress anyway.

What lost object is so important to cause hopelessness? We might feel sadness over losing an object of financial or emotional value, but isn't it really just a "thing?"

When I realize what is of true value, my panic:

- Turns to calm
- Turns into gratitude
- Dissipates or goes away

Therefore, panic is of value in our lives.

After all, if we didn't have panic, we'd never know calm.

An Ironic Way to Learn

My softball team was playing in the annual play-off tournament. The winning team would go on to the World Series.

I was very ambivalent about the whole thing. I had participated less than usual this season because I was pursuing other activities. The team itself had gone through a lot of changes, including conflicts, people dropping out for various reasons, and miscommunications. (A typical year of softball)

We almost dropped out of the playoffs because we didn't have enough people to field the team. I was fine with ending the season by forfeiting our last game and being done with softball for awhile. However, a couple of our injured teammates said they could play and we scrapped up a team for the playoffs at the last minute. I didn't want to play, but I couldn't back out and let the team down.

There was a chance of rain during the weekend and part of me hope for bad weather so the games would be cancelled! Instead, it was a beautifully sunny weekend, so we played. It was a double elimination tourney, so I figured we'd be done by early Saturday afternoon.

We won the tournament. We got to go to the World Series.

How did this happen?

I believe it came down to three things:

- We let go of the history of the season.
- We supported and encouraged each other. Every member of the team was vital, and we all knew it.
- We had fun!

The irony of my not wanting to play and our winning doesn't escape me.

The re-learning of things I already know to be true is reassuring; but experiencing those lessons in unexpected ways is magnificent.

To me this is winning.

Applause!

When I was growing up, my dad received a birthday gift from a family friend. It was a box on which were printed the words "Unappreciated? Underrated? Underestimated? Take A Bow!" When you opened up the box, you pressed a button. A flood of applause and screams of *more, encore, take a bow* and *bravo* filled the room.

For the next 20 years, whenever I went home, I asked my dad if I could take the box. He would say no! Finally, when my parents were moving to another home. Dad let me have his birthday present. I unabashedly admit from time to time I go to the box, push the button and take in all the applause.

How often do I readily acknowledge praise from others and most of all, from myself? I tend to get too embarrassed and self-conscious to accept the praise.

By accepting praise and applause it helps me:

- Be nicer to myself
- Get motivated to do what I want
- Feel damn good and special!

So I'll push the applause button whenever I can.

Babysitting

It was a running joke for my friend and me ever since he adopted his child. I kept saying I would love to baby sit but anytime he asked, I was unavailable.

Indeed, I really wanted to! It was on my to do list, my desire list, yet I could never get my schedule together to spend an afternoon or an evening sitting with the baby.

A few years went by. Still no babysitting.

I let it go; it wasn't on my list anymore.

One day my evening plans were cancelled. As I hung up the phone with the person who had to cancel, I briefly thought of what I might do instead.

No sooner did I hang up when the phone rang again. It was my friend wondering if there was any remote chance I might be free to baby sit that very night.

I said I would love to and asked what time I should be there.

This took him by surprise.

It took me by surprise as well.

My friend and his partner were able to do something fun for themselves, and I had a good time getting to know their son.

It couldn't have been planned any better.

Some things need to be planned. Some things are better left to happen when they happen.

When I'm able to let things happen when they happen:

- I save a lot of time in trying to plan something which won't work out in the present moment
- I stop hitting my head against a wall

- It all works out

How much time would be wasted if I wondered why I didn't baby-sit sooner? Why put pressure on myself wondering if I really wanted to baby-sit why hadn't done so already?

I let all those thoughts go, and it eventually happened.

And it'll happen again.

Banging My Elbow

I was having one of those days.

The computer was slow, a few appointments were cancelled, I hadn't slept well, I was behind in what I was doing, and I felt overwhelmed.

I wasn't happy.

Even worse, I was irritable and negative. Every thought I had was pessimistic and not motivating to me.

As I was heading into a downhill spiral, I accidentally banged my elbow against a corner of the desk.

Hard.

Very hard.

It hurt.

A lot.

Enough to make me stop.

I had to breathe. I needed to go and check to see what my elbow looked like. I had to stop and regroup.

Suddenly, I was no longer irritable and negative.

Banging my elbow shook me out of my negativity. It woke me up.

When I banged my elbow:

- I stopped the unconscious spinning of my mind.
- I was able to pause and breathe.
- I moved on.

Now, I don't want to have to be injured every time I need a reminder to not be irritable.

But the cost of a little momentary pain is worth the price of shifting my outlook from one of irritation to one of appreciation.

Howard Miller

Bank of America Screwed Me Over Again

I noticed my bank account balance was significantly lower than I thought it should be. My research showed me that Bank of America had deducted my credit card charge of $1900 -- twice. This accounted for the discrepancy.

I don't bank with this institution, since it screwed me over several years ago with a deposit I made. However, I retained a credit card sponsored by BofA because it offered a rewards program which sounded attractive to me.

I called customer service and spoke to a representative who was able to see the error. But, the $1900 was now $2900 since I had already accumulated an additional $1000 on my credit card.

So, I still had $1900 coming to me. It was my money, and I wanted it back.

Bank of America was capable of getting it back to me -- by writing a check and mailing it. I asked them why they couldn't directly deposit it into my account since they took the money directly from my account. They informed me that a direct deposit into my account would take a few days. However, they saw that I qualified to have the check sent via UPS, so I could receive it sooner (What?? -- They screw up, and I *qualify* for them to overnight a check! Should I feel grateful?)

At moments, when I focused on the situation, I felt powerless and angry. They made the mistake, they had my money, and I had to waste my time and lose interest on my money because of their mistake.

And there ain't nothing I could do about it!

In reality, there is something I can do. I don't have to use the card. I don't have to use this institution. I can share this mix-up with others and maybe they won't use this institution either.

Even though I didn't know the credit card was sponsored by Bank of America at the time I selected it, I returned to BofA as a customer because I felt I would benefit from the rewards program provided by the card.

Apparently, I needed to rethink this.

When I focus on what I can control versus what I cannot control:

- My anger lessens.
- I see alternatives.
- I take action.

Now if any of you know someone who works at Bank of America, feel free to pass this story along!

Being Bitter

I was inappropriate and flippant with someone I know. I didn't realize I was until I was talking to him weeks later, and he mentioned the incident.

I immediately recognized my behavior, owned up to it and profusely apologized. He said it wasn't an issue anymore. He also mentioned that he had figured I was bitter about something.

The word *bitter* stung me.

I didn't say anything to him, but I thought about it. I was resistant to the fact that I was bitter. I could accept being seen as judgmental or obnoxious, but not bitter!

Around the same time, I was having a conversation with someone else. I mentioned something he had said to me awhile back. He smiled, and casually apologized, and said he was bitter at the time!

Wow! He owned up to being bitter! I thought about it and my friend was right. I *was* bitter at the time!

I was resistant, because I felt bitter was such a strong word to describe how I was feeling at the time, and more importantly, *bitterness* seemed to be a more permanent state of being.

It was the second person who made me realize it was my interpretation of the word which kept me resistant. When I acknowledged my resistance, I was free to move on.

When I let go of my internal interpretations:

- I can accept feedback
- I am free to move on
- Everything is a little bit easier

When we accept bitter, we can also appreciate sweet.

Being In a Bad Mood

I was in a bad mood that lasted a few days. Maybe I got in this mood because my birthday was coming up, and I put too much meaning on it. Maybe it was the fog. Or,, perhaps it was for no particular reason at all. Nonetheless, I felt pretty low, low enough not to care about changing my mood.

I was leaving a client's office, still in the bad mood. When I got to my car, I found it blocked by a moving van. I had no idea how long the van would be there, and I didn't particularly want to find the driver. I had a list of errands to run in a short amount of time.

I started to get angry, and then thought, "Screw it! The gym is right there. I have my gym bag. I'll go work out, and the errands can wait."

I grabbed my bag, headed to the gym, and started working out. I started to smile as I was working out because I realized I was feeling better. I was amused to think if I had been in a good mood prior to finding my car blocked by a van, it might have shifted me to a bad mood, but since I was already in a bad mood, it seemed to work the other way!

I could say it was the exercise which put me in the better mood, but I had worked out a couple of times in prior days, and my mood hadn't shifted. I could surmise that maybe it was because I had taken control of the situation.

But the truth is I really don't know what had made me feel so low in the first place, and I don't know what turned my mood around. I do know that when I find myself in a bad mood, it won't last. I have *faith* my mood will turn around. Having *faith* won't change my mood immediately, but I know things will change in the not too distant future.

Howard Miller

Having this faith:

- Gives me the space to be in a bad mood.
- Gives me strength to ride out the bad mood
- Gives me the gift of knowing how much I'll appreciate my better mood

Being on Time

Now more than ever for me, being on time is vital in my business. I pace my clients with 5 to 15 minutes in between appointments. One client being late can cause the whole day to fall behind for me.

Being on time is a challenge for many people and has been for me many times in my life.

But the truth is, for me anyway, being on time is a choice. I can be on time if I know I have to.

I've asked many of my clients, "If you knew you would get one million dollars if you were on time what would you do to make sure you were not late?"

The responses ranged from arriving the night before to setting many alarms.

As manager of our softball team while we were in the World Series, I used the same example in trying to get everyone to the fields at the designated time.

One morning I was the first to arrive. I got to our fields and did some meditating and stretching. As I was stretching I happened to glance down on the ground, and right there was a ten dollar bill!

I had to laugh. While it wasn't one million dollars, I had a perfect, real example of what being on time can get you!

When I am on time for anything:

- I am prepared
- I am present
- I don't need to apologize

So perhaps you should try to be on time as much as possible.

Because you never know what you'll find when you get there.

Bringing vs. Going

I had arranged a conference call between my father, brother, and me to celebrate my dad's birthday. During the conversation, my upcoming trip to visit my folks with my niece came up. I mentioned I was *bringing* my niece to see my folks. My brother didn't like my saying this. He felt *bringing* implied I was taking her, versus saying I was *going* with her, which would put us more as equals.

Uh, she's six years old. (Sorry, 6 ½ according to my niece). I was *bringing* her.

I was responsible for her. I would have to deal with what would happen if she had to use the bathroom while at the airport. Or more likely if I had to use the bathroom.

If we were going as equals I wouldn't be standing backwards on the Starbucks line so I could see her at every moment while waiting to purchase a muffin.

If we were going as equals she would have bought me the *Polly Pocket dolls* at the Disney store in the airport instead of the other way around.

Bringing. Going.

Two different words.

I probably made more of a deal out of it since my brother brought it up. With others, I might have not noticed the difference.

We all use words thinking we all agree on the meaning only to discover a misunderstanding exists because something entirely different was meant.

One exercise I do in my workshops with managers involves identifying what words we all use frequently mean to them as individuals.

I have them write down words such as *always, sometimes, occasionally, frequently & never.* I then have them assign a number representing a percentage for each of the words, each number represents how they interpret the word. For instance, if someone says I *always* do something, does that mean they do something 100% of the time?

I <u>always</u> get different percentages and I have <u>never</u> gotten everyone to say 100% for <u>always</u> or 0 for <u>never</u>!

We all attach different beliefs and meanings to words. When I am aware of this fact:

- I am more careful when I choose words
- I ask questions of others to make sure I do understand what they mean
- My communication with others is clearer.

I still say I *<u>brought</u>* my niece to see my folks. The week had its challenges as well as moments I'll always treasure.

So I did *bring* my niece. But, I'm *going* to remember the adventure.

Calf Strain Optimism

I pulled my calf during a softball practice. I was running fast to catch a ball when suddenly I felt as if someone had thrown a rock and hit the back of my leg.

My calf swelled up.

At first, I was in denial. I wanted to go dancing that night; I hadn't gone in so long. Besides, how could this happen in a routine practice?

Fortunately, I stopped this way of thinking pretty quickly. I went home, iced up my knee, wrapped it, and elevated my leg. A friend came over to get my crutches and cane from my storage unit. Ten years prior, I had broken my *other* leg and luckily still had the crutches.

Because of this injury, I slowed down despite everything I *needed* to get done.

I know everything happens for a reason, and so far I've come up with two reasons this happened:

One is to make it clear to stop favoring my left leg. For 10 years I've been doing so - now I can't because this is the one injured.

The second reason is to slow down and enjoy each moment.

I know this. I write about this.

But I forget this - a lot.

This injury, which is very minor compared to the one I had before and compared to what could have happened, reminded me to slow down.

When I remember the value of slowing down:

- I'm breathing
- I'm grateful
- I'm appreciative

While I really truly would not have wanted to have this injury to be reminded of what's important, I am humbled and blessed for the reminder I apparently needed

Can I Be Honest with You?

In the 1991 movie *Other People's Money,* someone asks the slimy lead character, played by Danny DeVito - *Can I be honest with you?*

His response: *I hate that question. It means you're lying to me the rest of the time.*

I have a friend who uses this expression all the time. I know it's more of a colloquial phrase for him then anything else.

I recently had a business associate say this to me I was expressing interest and concern for his growing company. He used this phrase to preface his comments to me because he thought I might be put off by what he said.

In that moment, I realized people use this phrase when they feel vulnerable. They fear if they are honest the other person will get angry.

I rarely find this to be the case. Yes, sometimes there might be some initial anger on the other person's part. But, if the intent is to be truthful, ultimately the air is cleared by the honesty, bonds are strengthened, and a longer path of trust is created.

When a client or business associate asks *Can I be honest with you?*

- I feel complimented that they feel comfortable to be vulnerable in my presence
- My compassion automatically increases
- I become more understanding even if there is initial anger

When my friend says it to me, I laugh.

Can You Hear Me Now?

I'm a big fan of *24* starring Kiefer Sutherland. I love it for its non-stop action and great acting. Many of the plots are incredulous, but I get past what seems unrealistic and stick with the adrenaline rush.

Except for the cell phones.

On this show, cell phones work everywhere! In tunnels, underground, in lousy weather... Everywhere!

At times, I can't get *mine* to work right smack in the middle of town.

Cell phones have definitely changed accessibility in my life. But sometimes, I desire a little less accessibility.

Do I really need to check my messages as much as I do? Do I need to be talking to someone while I'm driving and know I will get disconnected anyway?

How many times have I found myself asking, *"Can you hear me now?"* and groaning as I say this trendy, overused tagline?

Not long ago, I spent the weekend in an area where my phone would not work. For the first few hours, I felt a little panicked and a little disconnected from the outside world. But soon, I appreciated not having to focus on something which wasn't happening in my immediate surroundings. I enjoyed being in the present moment instead of giving my attention to someone who was miles away.

Don't get me wrong. I'm not giving up my phone. Its usefulness is important to me. But I do find that the stress caused by this *convenience* makes my cell phone a bit *inconvenient* at times.

When I choose to use my cell phone less, even though it has value at other times:

- I give myself the opportunity to focus on the things which deserve my immediate attention
- I feel a little more sane!
- I realize there really isn't any material possession I can't live without

Too much of anything isn't good. Yes, my cell phone plan allows me absurd number of night and weekend minutes. But using them up is not my goal. There are better things to do.

Cellophane

Singing and performing have always been part of my life, and I have been fortunate to participate in many shows and singing groups throughout the years. I haven't performed much these last few years, but I have a few songs that I've done many times in various venues that I can pull out on different occasions.

One such song is *Mr. Cellophane* from *Chicago*. I've been singing it since way before the movie ever came out. (And between you and me, I wasn't thrilled by the way it was done in the movie!)

I had the opportunity to sing this song recently. However, I wasn't excited about the song – been there, done that.

About an hour before show time, I commented to a few people that singing the song yet again wasn't exciting to me. I joked that it might take actually singing the song while wrapped in cellophane to get me interested in singing.

"Why not do that?" I was promptly asked by one of my friends.

I paused.

Why not??

There was Saran Wrap available. I could figure out a way to get it on my body.

This would certainly be the first time I ever performed in Saran Wrap. It would bring a whole new meaning and interpretation to the song.

Would I dare?

You bet!

I sang *Mr. Cellophane*—wrapped in Saran Wrap!.

A song I love but was tired of singing became much more interesting when I added this element.

A flippant remark was taken seriously, and I had been challenged. Something ordinary and routine became a unique and pretty wild experience.

When things become humdrum, I can change them by challenging myself. I realize:

- Any moment can be made interesting
- Creating variety is easy.
- Life is for the taking

City Hall

I needed to go to city hall to process some paper work. I was a bit anxious about how long the process would take and wondered if I'd have to deal with any incompetence or red tape.

It all went smoothly.

Midway through completing my tasks, as I was walking from one room to another, I realized that it wasn't this task which needed to be changed; it was my attitude.

What would have happened if I had actually experienced delays or anything else I had anticipated?

My anticipation had already caused enough anxiety. Any true delay would have put me through the roof!

As it was, even though things were going smoothly, I was walking around expecting trouble.

When I realized it was my attitude which was the real problem:

- I walked slightly slower.
- I noticed the beautiful architecture of our city hall.
- I was friendly with everyone around me.

I still would rather have been able to do what I wanted online. Avoiding the trip to city hall altogether would have pleased me.

Nonetheless my shift in attitude made the experience more pleasant.

When we are brave enough to realize it's our attitude, above all else, which is in most need of change, making that change reduces stress and anxiety.

Even in the midst of red tape at city hall.

Howard Miller

Deck the Hall

Not *Deck the Halls.*

Deck the Hall.

I am Jewish from New York, and I know this. I grew up singing Handel's *Messiah, For unto Us a Child Is Born,* and Bach's *Kyrie Eleison,* along with the usual Christmas songs.

There is no *S* at the end of Hall.

Even so, someone always sings the *S.* And, all it takes is one person in the chorus to sing *halls* rather than *hall,* and it sounds like the entire chorus sang *halls.*

We're not singing about cough drops here.

We are all so used to hearing "Deck the <u>Halls, that</u> I have a feeling, that even if by some miracle no one in the chorus sang the word incorrectly, the audience would still hear it.

I had never been in a choir where the plural wasn't heard.

I would even remind my fellow singers right before we sang, and sure enough, at least one person would sing the plural.

Until last week.

A group of us who go to nursing homes, hospitals, hospices (and fun parties!) to perform Christmas carols were about to go on -- I jokingly reminded everyone that there is no *S* in *hall.*

We went up to sing....

And, we all sang HALL!!.

It was a miracle--a Christmas miracle!

I know there are serious consequences when a group or society changes something without consciousness or awareness. However, I find it comforting to know there are also times this happens where the change is simply funny.

When you can do something wrong with no consequences:

- It shows we don't always have to take ourselves seriously.
- It can be funny.
- It's a shocker when you do it right!

Happy Hanukah everyone! Or, is it Happy Chanukah?

Did I Do Enough?

My role as a Big Brother came to an end. I had participated in the program for almost seven years, although the last year had been pretty inconsistent.

The end left me with a mixture of emotions, including gratitude, sadness and relief. These emotions are natural after any relationship/partnership, with its many challenges and rewards, ends.

But what still gets me is that I continue to ask myself:

Did I do enough?

No answer serves me.

I'm left questioning everything I did. I'm left feeling *guilty* because I could always have done more.. *I'm left feeling overwhelmed and stressed..*

It's a bad question.

Questions which would serve me better and do more honor and justice to the situation include:

What did I learn?
What will I miss?
What would I have done differently?
What would I do the same?

Asking those questions encourages me to look at both the highlights and low points which I experienced in the Big Brother/Big Sister program.

When I ask those questions, I see things the way they were. I stay grounded, and I can feel gratitude, sadness and relief *without* feeling overwhelmed and stressed.

When I ask myself good questions in any situation:

- I figure things out
- I look at the situation realistically
- I learn

Bad questions keep me spinning. Good questions teach.

Doing My Own Taxes

I have my own business. I own a condo which I rent out. I convert IRAs to ROTH IRAs.

Naturally, I thought I could do my own taxes. After all I had the return from the year before. All I'd have to do is follow it, right?

Actually I didn't have these thoughts until a friend gave me TurboTax.

I thought since it was given to me, I might as well use it – I mean, how long would it take? Three, maybe five hours at the most?

I did bits and pieces here and there. But the final deadline for filing was coming up soon. I needed to get the work done.

So I spent a little more time –

And found I owed the federal government over $2000!

I freaked.

Then I realized I had forgotten to include the property tax I paid.

Whew!

So now I was down to about $700.

Better, but I didn't think I should owe *any* money.

And, shouldn't Turbo Tax have reminded me about paying property tax?

By accounting for a few more expenses that I had forgotten to record, I cut what I owed down a bit further.

At this point I was unsure if what I had done was accurate.

And all together I had spent about 6 hours on this, stressing continuously about getting everything right and finished.

One of my clients is a bookkeeper and tax preparer.

I took everything to her.

She looked at it for about 40 minutes.

I should get a refund close to $200!

How many times have I talked to my clients about delegating, about how it actually saves money to pay an expert to do something we don't need to do? Lots of times!!!

Yet, I didn't initially delegate myself.

When I do delegate:

- I can spend my time on what I do well
- I'm complimenting whomever I'm delegating to by trusting his or her experience
- I'm saving my time, my money, and my *sanity*

There is no question about who is doing my taxes next year!

Donna Summer Has No Rhythm

I won two tickets to see Donna Summer perform. I had never seen her and was excited to go. She sounded great. The concert was memorable, fun, current and relevant. She had a great stage show with dancers, musicians, and video.

She couldn't dance.

She couldn't even move *gracefully*.

How ironic that the woman who was instrumental in creating a new type of dance music (disco) couldn't keep the beat. The most she did was wave her arm up in the air a few times, trying to keep in time with the music.

I found this hilarious.

I also found it inspiring.

A woman who can't dance and has no graceful moves managed to help invent a type of music which revolutionized the 1970's music and dance scene.

What if Donna had let her lack of moves stop her from going into singing and specifically into singing music people dance to?

Sure the dance craze known as disco might have still happened, but how different it would have been?

This makes me think and inspires me:

- The fact that I procrastinate doesn't mean I can't motivate others.
- The fact that I might handle some of my own difficult situations ineffectively doesn't mean I can't show others how to shift out of these more efficiently
- The fact that I haven't gotten national recognition yet for my work doesn't mean my work and outcomes are any less relevant

Perhaps it's my own imperfections and the fact that I too struggle to live my life effectively that gives me the insight and empathy to coach others. Helping others also helps me to grow.

And *heaven knows*, if Donna can sing dance music even though she can't dance, the possibilities are endless for the rest of us!

Friends versus Acquaintances

At one point in my life I was concerned because I felt I didn't have many friends. I knew a lot of people and had lots of acquaintances, but not friends. Thinking about this would sadden me and make me worried and concerned.

I compared myself to others. I noticed how others seemed to have friends everywhere.

Why didn't I? What was wrong with me?

I suppose I eventually got bored with this type of thinking because it suddenly occurred to me I had definitions for a friend versus an acquaintance. And if I were comparing, according to other people, a lot of my acquaintances were friends.

So I started to think of these acquaintances as friends.

All of a sudden, I stopped comparing myself to others. I stopped wondering why I didn't have many friends because I was treating many more people as friends.

And I now had many friends.

Nothing changed except my perception. I changed my rules and restrictions and allowed what was happening to be the answer.

My old definition of friends didn't allow for many friends. This didn't make me happy.

My new definition allowed an overflow of friends which made me feel excited, welcomed and love.

When I create a reality for myself which excites me and makes me feel welcomed and loved:

- I am open to more of the unknown
- I am more adventurous
- I am friendlier and more open!

Why should you ever say you have <u>enough</u> friends? It's a great thing to have them in abundance.

Genius or Insanity?

I have a friend who, when in high school, was obsessed with the movie *Carrie*, starring Sissy Spacek. He saw it numerous times and knew all the words for most of the scenes and characters.

He worked part time at McDonalds. He confessed one evening he swiped a vat of ketchup from the store and brought it home.

When everyone was asleep, he went into the shower and dumped the ketchup on himself parodying the famous scene where the blood is dumped on Carrie at the prom.

My friend was embarrassed to reveal this story. (And would kill me if he knew I was writing about this experience.)

But when I heard this story I immediately thought what he did was brilliant!

He thought it was embarrassing.

What makes something brilliant or embarrassing? What makes it genius or insanity?

If my friend ends up poor and destitute and told the story it would be looked at as insane.

If my friend became famous and was being interviewed and told the very same story, it would be looked on as genius, as insight into the early years of a creative artist!

Society judges whether something is genius or insane based on circumstances which may have nothing to do with the original intent or idea.

We can't control what society judges.

But we can control how we feel about our ideas and intentions.

If we are embarrassed about an idea, the intent of the idea will never come to fruition.

If we support the ideas we have:

- We stand in our intention
- We are focused
- We nurture our creativity

Anyone obsessed with The Exorcist?

Get Out of My Way

I don't do well when I'm behind a slow driver.

I feel my patience is being tested.

I fail every time.

I feel I'm being punished when I'm behind the driver and can't get past them. I feel they are driving slowly on purpose. They are having a power trip and getting pleasure because I can't get past, and I'm getting angry.

I also know if my thought patterns were like this in other aspects of my life I would be put away.

I know road rage is common among many and this fact could give me comfort.

But I also know that these rash moments of irritation, frustration and anger aren't good for me.

I've tried not to get irritated but after all these years the habit is hard to break.

So I stopped trying to avoid getting aggravated.

Instead after my ranting – either to myself or out loud (usually when no one else is in the car, although others have seen this insane part of me) –

I pray for them.

So it goes something like this:

You son of a b*tch, get out of my f**ken way. And god bless you!

It helps!

My irritation, frustration, and anger lasts a shorter amount of time and is diminished.

For years I tried stopping this habit completely. It didn't work.

When I didn't stop the habit, but added to it.

- It changed the habit
- It produced a more desired effect
- It greatly reduced my irritation, frustration and anger.

I don't know if I'll ever be a calm driver. But I do believe this practice can help me go from an insane crazy driver to a semi-frustrated one. This is progress!

Getting Invited to Parties with My Old Email Address

I have one friend who has not updated his email address book, so every time he invites me to something, using Evite, I don't get the invitation right away.

The invitation is there in the Evite system, but I don't get an email telling me about it since it's using an older email account I don't check frequently.

I've tried to get my friend to update his address book, but to no avail. It's frustrating to me.

Lately, I've realized my frustrations is a little ridiculous.

How would I feel if he didn't invite me at all?

What is the real problem of not knowing about an invitation immediately? I always get the invite before the event happens.

So, is it more important to be picky about when and how I get the invite? Or, would I prefer to get no invite at all?

When I shift my priorities to what's important I immediately go from needing to be right to being grateful.

When I get into this gratitude:

- I see things more clearly.
- I receive what is really important.
- I embrace imperfection.

How lucky I am to have friends who invite me to events, parties, and dinners!

How grateful I am to have people in my life who care about me.

This is indicated to me by their actions.

An administrative glitch is only a glitch.

An invitation is an indication of friendship.

Getting What You Want in a Way You Didn't Think You Could!

I love getting massages. I find them very relaxing, centering, healing, and one of the best ways to relieve my stress.

When I started my own business, the frequency of my massages dropped. While I wanted the massages, it wasn't where I chose to spend my money at the time. I know massage should be a necessity, but I look at it as a luxury.

So, I have bartered coaching for massage! Instead of paying each other cash, the massage therapists and I each provide a service to help the one another.

In my case, I'm helping massage therapists grow their businesses. And, they are helping me get more connected with myself.

So now I get more massages than I have ever gotten before!

It is amusing to me that while I am making less money than I did in the corporate world, I am getting more massages than I did in the past.

This has happened because I found a way to get what I want.

There's more than one way to skin a cat, so the saying goes.

If I really want something, I will get it.

When I realize I can achieve the end results I want in creative ways that I haven't even begun to imagine

- I am reminded that what I focus on is what I'll get
- I can let my imagination run wild without needing to edit the ideas
- The sky is the limit!

Glad to Be Sad

For the last two years there were four of us who met on a weekly basis. We would share what was going on for us, both personally and professionally. Each of us would have our turn to speak, and the others would have time to give feedback on what we said. It was a wonderful opportunity to put things in perspective and get things back on track when told we were crazy!

Now after two years, the group has ended. While we all valued this process tremendously, it started to become a hassle. Two members of the group had moved to new locations which involved fighting commuter traffic when we met. The weekly event became an all evening program. While it was nice to see everyone and I always felt better at the end of the evening, many times it was logistically difficult to pull together.

We all felt this way and decided we needed to end. After we decided to end we gave it some space and a couple of more weeks of meetings to provide closure.

At the final meeting, someone shared how they were feeling nostalgic, and almost sad. But there was apprehension in saying he was sad.

It was if by saying *he was sad, he was implying that* we were making the wrong decision by ending the group.

But it was sad to end.

Sad doesn't mean wrong. It doesn't mean right. It means sad.

It can be uncomfortable.

But it can be validating as well.

What we all shared and experienced was powerful, life changing, and validating.

We honored this by taking additional time to formally end the group.

We can be excited and nervous about not knowing what happens after.

And we can be sad for giving up something meaningful.

When we recognize our sadness:

- We give honor to the experience
- We remember the importance and minimize the inconveniences
- We value being happy much more

So, I was glad to be sad. It showed respect and reverence for something which deserved both.

Going to the Chapel

I've always dreaded weddings! I have never liked going to them. I find them rather irksome, boring, obligatory, and self-serving. If I were the one being served, that would be one thing, but they always seem self-serving to the people throwing the party. Go figure!

With the exception of my brother's wedding, I have always gone to weddings with an air of looking at the event as something I'd rather not do, rather than being open to the experience of what could be.

That all changed when I went to the wedding of two of my friends. I met both of them as a couple and became friends with them together and individually. The event took place over a weekend. I was surrounded by them, their family, and a lot of my other friends.

Instead of going to places of jealousy, contempt, boredom, or sarcasm, I accepted the love which was all around during the weekend. There was love everywhere! We were all there to celebrate the union of two special people, our love for them, and the love we all shared for one another.

When I accepted love, and not the other noise in my head:

- I was closer to my true self
- I was totally in the magic
- I saw all that is possible for me in my life

Finding love brings out the love within. The result of love is more love. Not a bad deal.

Going with the Flow

I was teaching a workshop for the IRS, something I had done many times before. The workshop was entitled *How to Deal with Difficult People.* Again, this is something I had taught many times.

I was teaching in an auditorium since there were over 100 attendees. The people in this audience were the employees who spend eight hours a day answering phone calls from people who owe the IRS money.

I assumed the callers were the difficult people.

Shortly after I started my presentation, an attendee raise her hand and asked, *"What if we felt the difficult people weren't the people calling in, but our managers?"*

The entire auditorium erupted with applause. I felt like a revolution was about to start.

My first reaction was:

They're not paying me enough to have to deal with this!

But to have ignored this shift by the majority of the audience would have been an insult and anything else I had to say would have been dismissed.

So this workshop I had done many times before took a new twist.

I let them vent for about five minutes -- this is when they started repeating themselves. At this point, I wrote down the highlights of their gripes.

Throughout this process, while they were venting, I also made sure they were laughing by keeping it light hearted.

Once we had the highlights written down I turned the tables and had them see where they were being difficult and what they could do to have better relationships with their managers.

At the end of the session everyone thanked me and hoped I would be back soon to run other meetings. Admittedly, this feedback felt great!

But the truth was it was simple for me to do and the main reason it was simple:

I went with the flow.

I didn't fight what was happening, I accepted it.

Whenever I go with the flow in any aspect of my life:

- Things go more smoothly
- There is less stress
- There is more humor

This is consistent. This is easy.

Except when it isn't. Then, I'm swimming upstream.

I'd rather go with the flow.

Guilt, Obligation or Because I Want To?

I was on vacation in Florida visiting my parents, a good friend, and friends I had yet to meet.

When I left my parents for what was the last night, my parents were taken a little aback. "Is that all? You only spent a few nights here and were out most of them!"

I held my ground and <u>did</u> leave.

A few days later on my way from one friend's house to another I felt uncomfortable. I wasn't sure what it was. I realized I felt funny about not seeing my parents once again before I left Florida.

How often am I close enough to where they are that I can drop in and hang out for a few hours?

The next morning I called them to see what they were doing for dinner. I ended up going to their house for dinner on my last night, and then went back to my friends which was closer to the airport.

Was it guilt which made me want to see them again?

Did I feel obligated to see them?

Or did I want to?

Who cares?

All I know, for whatever reason, *I didn't feel right. I didn't feel comfortable.* When I acknowledged these thoughts I acted on them and felt better.

When I am true to my feelings instead of wondering why I'm having them:

- I am being honest

- I am able to act on my feelings
- I'm moving forward in my life, not staying stuck in my emotions

Making decisions can be difficult. What makes them less so for me is if I pay attention to how I feel after I've made them. If I don't feel right, how wonderful that I can admit that the decision doesn't sit right with me, and then change my decision.

Having to Reschedule an Entire Day

As a consultant I have various employers – my coaching clients, companies where I do contract work, and companies where I have ongoing projects.

On one particular day, there was a slim chance that I would be teaching a workshop. Because this was only a slim chance, I scheduled a couple of other meetings for the day. Soon, I had forgotten all about the workshop, so I booked the entire day.

That slim chance workshop became a sure thing!

It was a go.

Since I had agreed to it, I needed to fulfill the obligation.

I had to spend time moving all the other appointments to other days. This took my time with emails and phone calls. In order to accommodate the changes, I also had to juggle other activities which weren't as vital on other days.

This process aggravated me. Not everyone was available to talk when I called or to respond to email immediately.

My schedule was in flux, and I wanted it to be stable.

I realized how ridiculous I was being.

A couple of years before, when starting out in business, I would have loved to have had the problem of having to reschedule some clients because I had a workshop to teach.

Now I had the problem and was complaining about it.

Yes, it can be a scheduling nightmare, and it can take time to make the changes. But, when I look at those logistics from a place of success:

- I don't berate myself
- The aggravation is worth the effort
- I feel rewarded

I'm not saying I will purposely double book to reward myself.

But isn't it more comforting and inspiring to see changing appointments as a sign of success instead of seeing it as lack of organization.

Hurricane Wilma

Don't I mean Katrina? No, I mean Wilma. This one held my attention for two reasons which hit closer to home: my parents.

They live in DelRay Beach Florida, north of Fort Lauderdale.

I expressed my concerns about the hurricane before it hit Florida.

My parents are both native New Yorkers. They were raised, went to school, and had children in New York. Up until a few years ago they had always lived in New York. As far as they're concerned, Florida is New York South. Most of their childhood friends are there. Relatives they haven't seen in years are there. Old neighbors and teachers I had are there.

So my parents had typical New York reactions to the pending hurricane.

Mom: *"I'm not thinking about it now; I'm heading to the movies."*
Dad: *"Can we talk about something else? We'll deal with it if it gets here."*

I pressured my mom to fill the car with gas. I wanted them to get some groceries – Mom said they were fine - they had water and beer for my dad.

I pictured a report from CNN – "local Florida residents prepare for the hurricane. The Smith family board up their windows. George Miller, 83, from DelRay Beach, bought beer."

The hurricane hit harder than expected.

I managed to get through to them as the hurricane was happening.

Mom said the noise of the wind was unbelievable. She had never heard anything like it before. Both my parents were staying away from the windows and had to soak up the water that was coming through the front door.

They were very lucky. While damage was done all around them, they escaped with only a few cracked window panes. They even got power back a few days after the storm since they are on the same grid as a nearby hospital.

I sense in my parents renewed thanks when they talk about the hurricane's destruction.

All of us focused on how thankful we were for what didn't happen, as opposed to the damage and inconvenience.

When we are thankful we are experience:

- Humility
- Gratitude
- Appreciation for what we have

I know my parents (and I) will continue to have a certain stereotypical *New York Edge*.

But it's great to know this edge also includes the qualities of humility, gratitude, appreciation, thanks and beer.

I Couldn't Find Parking Because of the Toilet Sale

We were having our softball playoffs. We had played at these particular fields before so I gave the proper time to drive over, find parking and head to the fields.

There was no parking.

Instead there were mobs of people surrounding a bunch of toilets.

Apparently, our gas and electric company has an annual toilet sale, where they sell water-saving toilets at reasonable rates. Evidently, this annual event is quite popular.

Of course, I wasn't the only one late because of the lack of parking due to the toilets sitting in the parking spots. Everyone was.

Remembering this day makes me laugh!

I love when things in life happen which are so outrageous you couldn't even think of making them up!

Even as I was driving around looking for parking, I was laughing because I knew I couldn't find parking because of a toilet sale.

When I see the humor in events which could be stressful:

- I'm living more in the here and now
- I'm taking what life has to offer
- I know I can't predict all of life's possibilities

And this flushes out negativity!

I Didn't Know People Your Age Make Mistakes

I made an error in judgment. I did something stupid. I regretted it and knew there would be consequences. I decided to accept the consequences, learn from them, and move on.

I still felt bad the evening of the mistake. At my chorus practice I requested hugs from various members. A younger woman in the chorus asked me what happened and I told her I had made a bad choice earlier in the day. Her sincere response to me was:

Wow I didn't realize older people made mistakes. Nice to know.

Ouch. Ow. Older. Yikes.

Stab me while I'm already wounded!

Yes I am a bit older than she is, old enough to be her... her older brother.

But still.

After I got over the fact that I am older I thought about the comment and the beliefs we might have.

When I'm older things will be perfect.

Owning a home will make me happy.

When I'm settled down everything will be alright.

We all have millions of beliefs, many of which don't serve us at all.

My bad choices and more importantly owning up to them can help others realize that mistakes can happen at any age. By sharing my mistakes, maybe I can help others have a fuller life because their expectations for themselves can be more gentle, caring, and human.

Knowing this makes me realize:

- Owning up to my actions not only affects me but sets an example for others
- Admitting my faults can be a service to others
- The importance of judging the actions of others the way you would want to be judged for your actions

These are beliefs that serve me at any age.

I Hate Insurance!

I hate it when I get a big envelope from my insurance company. I know it means yet another increase to my monthly premium (which has doubled in the last two years.)

Recently, one of those envelopes was recently in my mail when I got back from vacation.

I immediately got resentful, felt ripped off, and hopeless because there was nothing I could do about the increase (besides trying to find another insurance company).

I became overwhelmed thinking of ways to resolve the insurance issues here in this country.

I also started wondering if I should go and get a full time job which includes insurance.

All this from receiving an envelope from my insurance company.

I hadn't even opened it.

Well, the envelope contained correspondence telling me about changes to my insurance plan – and I would receive the rate change in the near future.

Great, now I can dread getting a small envelope from the insurance company.

I have to laugh when I think about the immediate conclusion I make whenever I get something in the mail from the insurance company. It really emphasizes the power of focus.

Whatever we focus on, we get back. If I focus on resentment, I get resentment.

If I focus on gratitude (in this case I'm healthy and I hardly use my insurance) I achieve peace.

When I realize that what I focus on is what I will get back:

- I accept all my emotions
- I know I can switch from resentment to gratitude (or the other way around) in a second
- Things don't have to stay the same

By changing focus, a difficult situation can become an amazing experience.

This is the power of focus.

But, I still hate insurance.

I'm Glad You Were Here

A surprise 40th birthday party was being held for someone I've known for a number of years. While I don't see this person often I made definite plans to get to this celebration.

An event such as this makes us all think of our mortality and where we are in relation to celebrant.

I was flattered when a few people asked me if I had celebrated my 40th birthday.

Unfortunately, the guest of honor brought me back to earth when he told me my 40th party was the first he had ever attended.

Ugh!

OK. That's life.

At the end of the night when I left the party he said *I'm glad you were here.*

I thought of the power of this statement.

Each of us has effects on others we would never imagine. These effects can be both favorable and unfavorable. Often the same action can produce different results with different people or under different circumstances.

But how often do we acknowledge others?

Or rather, how much do we hear others acknowledging us?

It happens all the time. With a thank you, a smile, or a hello!

When I am open to hearing acknowledgement from others:

- I give more acknowledgement to others in return
- I am letting my intuition lead the way
- I am inspired

And age matters none!

Well, not as much!

I Went to Feed the Fish but Missed

My brother and nieces were visiting and staying at my place. On Sunday morning my eldest niece came into my room. I was half asleep and she said: *Uncle Howard I tried to feed the fish but missed.*

I was now wide awake.

I went with her into the living room. Sure enough there was fish food on the carpet and around the fish tank, but not in the fish tank.

The thing is the fish tank is out of her reach. I am tall enough to feed the fish but to clean the tank I need a chair to reach inside. Since my niece is only five, she would need a chair to feed the fish. She had managed to move the chair to the tank, stand on the chair, and pour some food into her hand. She wasn't tall enough to reach the top of the tank which is why the food went everywhere but the tank.

How easy it could have been to get irritated or annoyed. But no one told her not to feed the fish. No one told her she wouldn't be able to it on her own.

She tried a seemingly difficult task for her – while she didn't meet with the success she wanted she got a lot closer to the goal than I would have expected.

So I turned to her and smiled and said: *Wow! You moved the chair to the tank. Great job!*

I then lifted her up to feed the fish.

It did leave me wondering:

As an adult, how often have I not attempted something difficult because I was afraid of repercussions or criticism?

When I try for something which I'm seemingly unlikely to achieve:

- I move past my fear
- I embrace the unknown
- I associate with the beauty of trying for something despite the odds

And it took a five year old to remind me of this.

Intuition

I had my recent hand surgery done by the doctor who gave me a second opinion. I didn't plan on having him do the surgery but there was something about our meeting which got me to switch from the original doctor to him.

I mentioned this to my physical therapist early on in my healing process. She told me, (in confidence), I made a very wise decision. She knows most of the hand doctors in the city and the doctor who performed my surgery was on the A list; the original doctor didn't even make the D list!

I was taken aback when I heard this. What a lucky break! My expedited healing and recovery may have taken a different turn if I went with the original doctor.

There was something about the original doctor which didn't feel right to me. And, I went with the feeling.

This is the feeling of *intuition*.

Intuition is not fear. *Intuition* doesn't hold me back. *Intuition* is the voice deep within me, the true voice which, when I listen, leads me down the path of success.

When I listen to my *intuition*:

- I'm listening to what is going on around me, not what is going on in my head!
- I'm thinking with my heart
- I'm centered in trust, not fear

Who knows how the surgery and healing process would have gone with the original doctor? I don't need to go down this thought path. But it's nice to be able to say now, a little sooner than I thought, *tennis anyone?*

If You Believe It, It Will Happen!

When my dad turned 83 he admitted, while being healthy, he didn't play handball anymore.

Who is he kidding; he hasn't played in 50 years.

I asked him to what he attributes his health. He jokingly said my mom would get angry if he got sick. But then he mentioned how he always says he'll live to 120. And if he believes it, it'll happen.

While I think genetics, health, luck and physical fitness play into longevity, my father hit on what might be the most important element: your attitude and outlook.

In fact, our attitude and outlook affects everything we do, at any age. I know when I believe things are going to work out, they work out. I know, as well, when I get in a bad mood, I am more likely to notice what's going wrong and not see the great things in my life.

Numerous books have been written about having a great attitude and outlook. For me, it comes down to one simple and powerful fact: *If you believe it, it will happen.*

When I believe great things will happen in my life:

- My smile is brighter
- I feel a glow of gratitude within
- Things happen!

I haven't thought about where I'll be in 37 years .But, if my dad is here, I will be here as well!

I believe it!

It's How You View It

I have a client who resides in England. We have developed a rapport so when I coached him on July 5 and he asked me how I was, I was able to jokingly say

Great. I spent yesterday celebrating freeing ourselves from you

His response was

You mean when we gratefully got rid of you"

We both laughed and went on with our session. But I thought about this later.

Didn't we grow up learning we had a revolution and won the war and became independent? Yet, this *fact* is looked at differently in England – they had an unappreciated and ungrateful child who they let go.

Which one is true? Does it matter?

If in fact we *won,* and they *lost,* I doubt I would have a client in England. Yes I know this was over 200 years ago, but resentments and feuds can go on for generations and centuries.

What matters is honoring that there are different ways to view a situation.

If I don't get a particular business deal, what did I get?

If a relationship doesn't work out, what did?

When I see that there are different ways to view a situation:

- I look at situations in different ways
- I welcome diverse opinions
- I see failure as success

And, just for the record, we did win.

It's True: What Goes Around Does Come Around!

As an avid fan of *24* I never miss an episode. I don't watch the show live; I always watch it later because I record the show.

I have a circle of friends and family who also watch. They are under strict instructions to say nothing about the show unless I have said I watched it. Well at least one of my friends and my mother have these instructions because they are the ones I feel would reveal plot twists and surprises and ruin it for me.

My instincts weren't correct.

Another friend, who watches *24*, was casually talking to me a day after an episode aired and said "Can you believe they killed *****?" I was in shock they killed this character off, but more in shock that my friend had told me.

I really couldn't believe my friend would blurt this out – how insensitive.

A few months later, I was at his house and noticed, from his TIVO, that he watched *The 4400*. This is another show I watch, and I hadn't realized that my friend also watched the show.

I exclaimed surprise that he watched the show as well. He said he really enjoyed it – I mentioned I couldn't believe they killed off *** in the first episode of the current season.

He hadn't watched that episode yet.

The circle was complete.

I didn't do this on purpose. I was in the moment, as I understand now, he had been when he had blurted out a plot twist in 24 and had spoiled the surprise.

Both of us were laughing pretty hard at this and I believe he was somewhat relieved that I couldn't hold the *24* slip over him anymore.

When the shoe is on the other foot I realize:

- I should only judge someone the way I would want to be judged
- Until I experience something, I don't know how I'd react
- It all works out; it really does!

If my friend and I watch other shows in common, we don't talk about them. We keep our conversations to lighter subjects, like politics.

Kind Acts

I was at the Los Angeles zoo with my parents, brother and niece. To get to the top section of the zoo there is a tram you can take for an extra charge. The people in front of us were a couple of dollars short. When my brother found out, he said we would pay. He got the money from my father and gave it to them.

I was a little taken aback at my brother volunteering my father's money. I didn't say anything, nor did my parents.

It was our turn to pay and the woman at the ticket booth told us she rewarded acts of kindness and gave us all complimentary tickets.

My brother goaded me a little because he knew what I was thinking (hey, he's known me for a while.)

I admit I was stopped by what happened. I was witness to what had become a cliché for me. Actually, several clichés! *What goes around comes around, Do onto others*

Initially I was embarrassed because I wouldn't have paid the money for the strangers in front of us. I wouldn't have done the "right" thing.

Ultimately I went from embarrassment to the lesson which I always need to learn:

What you place out in the world is what you'll get back.

One kind act to strangers initiated another kind act to my family.

If I want more kindness (really, more of anything) all I need to do is put it out there. It will come back.

Howard Miller

When I realize this it makes me feel:

- Purposeful
- Powerful, because I have a choice about how I want to be in front of others.
- Hopeful to know how you treat others is the way you can be treated as well.

Initial embarrassment is worth the lessons it teaches.

Laughing at the Irony

I was giving a workshop at a government agency in Oakland, California.

I had talked with the coordinator and was to meet a representative of the company in a conference room near the cafeteria.

When I got there I had to go through security. I wasn't aware of this so my Swiss army knife presented a problem. Security wouldn't hold the knife for me (they would confiscate it) and since I took the train, I couldn't place it in my car. The security officers suggested I hide it in the bushes out front, which I did.

With that little crisis out of the way I proceeded to the conference room near the cafeteria.

No one was there.

I tried calling the coordinator but got their voice mail.

Finally a woman appeared who was coming for the workshop. A few others also appeared moments later.

We all weren't sure if the room we were in was the correct conference room since the materials for the workshop weren't there. Also, there was music being piped in and we couldn't figure out or get anyone to shut it off.

It didn't matter because half way through the workshop we had to leave the room since some other group had reserved the room.

We all went to a table in the cafeteria to finish the workshop.

The workshop?

Effective Communications.

The irony of the topic and the circumstances for the workshop didn't escape any of us.

Instead of griping about it, we laughed about it. We were able to use the experience as a topic for the workshop. It enhanced the learning.

When we were able to laugh at the irony instead of getting upset:

- We were uplifted by the humor
- It created an environment for growth and expanded thinking
- We got the most out of the workshop

The workshop ended up (in my opinion) better then if it had gone as planned.

And my Swiss army knife was right where I left it when I went to pick it up.

Laughing Out Loud While Alone

I don't know how the topic came up, but a friend of mine was surprised I laugh out loud when I'm alone.

I was surprised he didn't!

I always laugh out loud if something is funny! I don't need anyone around to hear me laugh!

I probably have laughed as much while by myself as I do with others.

There have been countless times watching television or movies where I find something funny. My laughter is automatic.

I was fortunate to grow up in a house where laughter was as strong a presence as any other emotion or way of expression. The book *Laughter is the Best Medicine* by Sam Levinson was a constant in my dad's bathroom library collection.

My parents' unique sense of humor definitely impacted me.

While our taste for comedy is quite different these days (I don't see what is so funny about *Everyone Loves Raymond* and my father can't get past the language in *South Park* to see any humor!) I recall their openness for laughter. I remember being at movies where the only two people laughing, at least out loud, were my parents.

So I laugh out loud as well!

When I laugh out loud even though I'm alone:

- I'm valuing myself as a whole, not depending on others
- I'm expressing myself
- I am instantly full of joy, happiness and wonder!

I can easily beat myself up when I'm alone. So why not laugh as well?

Laying All the Cards on the Table

The training project where I spend a large part of my time is very rewarding yet also demanding.

The intensity can get very high as you have to make decisions about letting employees go. We never want to let them go but sometimes need to do so when keeping them wouldn't benefit the client who hired us.

I was in a situation where I had a make a decision about someone -- I felt pressure (which was coming from within).

My colleague for whom I had great respect was sitting next to me. She already stated this person should go and was waiting for my decision.

What I wanted to say to her was I need a little bit of time to breathe and reflect so I can make the decision.

Instead what I said was:

Do you want me to make a quick decision so you can get to yoga on time?

She immediately looked at me and said

I work very hard on this project and I'm really insulted you would say this to me.

I saw she was upset and immediately realized what I had said.

I knew I was wrong. I owned it. I immediately apologized.

My colleague and I talked about this moment the next day. If this had happened a few years before the situation would have taken a very different turn. She wouldn't have said anything; instead she would have kept the anger within. I wouldn't have remembered the incident and realized what a ridiculous and rude statement I had made.

The result would have been a distance in the friendship which we had developed.

But because she spoke up and laid all the cards on the table, our friendship and business relationship is even stronger.

What happened was definitely uncomfortable.

But we always run across situations which can be uncomfortable. How we deal with them is what's vital.

If we ignore them, they will fester and grow.

It's a matter of respect to us and to the other person to tell the truth and lay it all on the table. It might be uncomfortable It may not be popular, but the results will be an outcome that is worthy of everyone involved.

When we lay our cards out on the table:

- We command respect for ourselves and for the other person
- We dive right into being uncomfortable which helps us release anger and disappointment
- We can laugh at something which could have kept us angry for years

As I get older, I don't want to waste my time, on negativity, especially with people I care about. I hope to be able to communicate my disappointments with gratitude and respect. I especially hope others will do the same with me.

Let It Go and It Will Come to You!

Several years ago, I used to worry about whether I'd be invited to parties. I'd spend a lot of time focusing on what events were happening, why it was important for me to be invited, and figuring out how I could be invited, or with whom I could tag along.

As the years have gone on, I simply stopped caring about whether or not I would be invited to parties.

This struck me as ironic a few weeks ago as I was rushing from one party to another.

Why is it that something I once considered vital, important, and crucial didn't show up in my life until I stopped focusing on it?

I believe it's because I was focusing on what wasn't happening in my life, instead of sitting in the possibility of what I wanted.

Although I did it unconsciously, when I stopped focusing on why I was NOT invited to parties:

- My expectations changed so I could appreciate a single invitation, instead of wishing there were more.
- I stopped setting myself up for failure because no matter how many parties I was invited to, it never was enough, and I was never satisfied.
- I was able to concentrate on what I did want in my life instead of what I wasn't getting.

Focusing on what I don't have in my life, (whether its time, money, success, a job, a relationship, or parties!) is a trap, a setup which sabotages me from getting what I deserve.

I try to live in my possibilities, not the lack thereof. If it's meant to be, I will get it!

Letting Go of My Entitlement

I had a falling out several years ago with someone who had been a pretty good friend. It never got resolved.

Recently, when I was out of town, waiting for a return flight home, this person happened to be waiting for the same flight.

I immediately wanted to avoid him.

He waved to me.

I acknowledged him – as he was boarding the flight, he said he would save a seat for me. (Southwest airlines!)

I took the seat hesitantly.

I realized I had a choice. I could hold on to the past and be right, or stay in the present.

I chose the latter.

I had a good conversation with him.

When we parted ways my spirits were up and I felt a little lighter.

When I let go of my entitlement

- I feel free
- I'm not living in the past
- I am more alive

It's much easier for me to live without all the gook (for want of a better word) then giving it life in me.

When I keep it alive I'm really not living.

Lost in the Attic

In the early years of the daytime soap opera *All My Children*, there was a teenage boy who was a member of one of the families on the show. At one point, he went up to the attic to get his skis. He never came down. The writers had written him out of the show, and no one mentioned him again.

I was dating someone for about a month. Things were going well. Then, it stopped. No phone calls, nor were my calls returned.

I guess they got lost in the attic.

For me it's disrespectful, and makes me sad and hurt when something like this happens. However I don't wish to go to anger or righteous indignation. It doesn't serve me.

Although I may want to try and understand what happened, if I did anything *wrong*, to get into their mind to *figure it out*, it doesn't work. It's impossible to do. Without a conversation, it's not an option.

When something happens to me which makes no sense and can't be figured out:

- I feel my true feelings, in this case being hurt and sad, and move on.
- I appreciate all the support I have from others and how much greatness I have going in my life.
- I keep wishing this other person well. If I keep wishing it, eventually I'll mean it.

There will always be relationships, experiences, incidents which get lost in the attic.

What gives me comfort is to know how much of my life is spent in the warmth of the living room.

Loving Something I Once Dreaded

When I first started playing softball I hoped the ball wouldn't come to me. I dreaded the anxiety I had in anticipation of a ball being hit to me in the outfield.

Now I love it.

What keeps me playing softball year after year is this realization.

When I'm in the outfield I go after everything. I run forward and backward to get to the ball. Many times my efforts result in a great but failed attempt, but many times I get the ball as well.

I can think of no greater high than jumping outwards for the ball and catching it.

Except maybe running far in and scooping the ball.

Or getting the ball on a bounce and throwing the ball infield, holding the batter to a single or double when, if the ball had gone past me, the hit surely would have been a home run.

Or running backwards for the ball, catching it and having everyone cheer.

When I'm in the outfield, I'm ageless. I'm without limits.

I wouldn't have anticipated this when I first started playing.

Realizing something I'm currently doing which causes me anxiety may be a huge source of happiness in the future:

- Gives me the resolve to continue
- Keeps me going when I'm struggling
- Makes me grateful for the true benefits of what I'm doing

Moments of anxiety and moments of exhilaration have more in common than I thought. To know there is commonality between them shows how we can love things we had once dreaded.

Making a Fist

There was an episode in the original *Star Trek* series where some evil presence was able to wipe out people's brains. Lieutenant Uhura fell under the spell of that evil presence. Through the episode, we saw the lieutenant acting like a baby, learning how to talk, and then learning how to read and write and getting excited by the process. Lieutenant Uhura had to relearn things she had known all her life and had taken for granted.

With my hand recovering from a recent surgery, it was time to begin physical therapy. Like ten years prior when I had to learn how to walk again after a tibia/fibula fracture, I was amazed by the simple ordinary functions I took for granted every day and now had to relearn.

Making a fist, a quick fast movement I had done throughout my life without about a thought, was now part of my daily workout regiment.

My initial therapy began with making a fist 20 times every hour. The first repetition was the hardest and required the use of my other hand to complete the fist. By the last repetition, it was slightly easier.

However, when it came time to do the exercise again the next hour, the first repetition was hard again, making it seem like I hadn't done it the hour before.

But I persisted.

Gradually, it got a little easier each time.

At this writing, I still have weeks to go but the daily regiments yield gradual healing.

My faith in the physical therapy is solid. My trust in the process is as well; I'm following directions, and not being willful and trying to do things (such as lifting weights) before its time.

When my faith is solid, and I trust the process:

- I don't procrastinate, I do what's required
- I have serenity because I'm focused in the moment
- I have respect for the power of time and patience.

I am excited because I figured out how to do push-ups with eight fingers!

Making Do with What You Have

I went to the gym after a client meeting and before going home for some client calls. At the gym I discovered I hadn't brought any white socks. The socks I had on were dress socks and wouldn't be appropriate with sneakers.

Okay, I can work out without socks, not a big deal I thought.

Then I realized I hadn't brought a shirt!

It wouldn't be appropriate to work out without a shirt.

I thought of what I would do and realized I had been wearing a tee shirt under my sweater. This shirt would be fine. I could get another tee shirt at home for when I went out that night.

So my workout continued as planned.

As I was working out, I realized how adaptable and flexible I was with the changes in my typical habits.

There are many times when I've made do with what I had, when I was adaptable and flexible.

When I spent six months backpacking through New Zealand, Australia, Bali and Thailand I had to be ready for changes and strategic about using what I already had on me in many situations.

In difficult work situations, I need to be adaptable to maintain good relations with the clients.

When things aren't going the way I want them to go, I need to make do. And if I don't, trouble will brew!

When I can make do with what I have, and be adaptable and flexible, no matter what the situation is:

- I'm being accepting instead of being willful
- I'm allowing change to happen in my life
- I'm growing as a person

When everything has to be perfect I'm so stressed on maintaining perfection instead of being in the moment.

Making do with what I have, being adaptable and flexible lets me stay open and see the opportunities in the present moment.

Missing the Turn

My co-worker and I were heading to the site where our training was being held – we'd been going to the same place for several weeks already.

We were in an animated discussion when she said to me (I was driving) *"Wasn't that where we turn?"* I was too busy talking and had missed it.

Slightly embarrassed, but mostly undaunted, I took the next turn.

It turns out this turn was more direct to where we wanted to go!

For the rest of the project, we took this new turn.

While it wasn't a major difference, we never would have learned about this new turn if I hadn't mistakenly skipped our usual left. We had taken the usual left, not only for weeks, but also last year, because this is what we learned.

How often do I do what has become usual instead of trying something new?

It's exciting to think a small thing, such as turning on a different street or walking down a different block can make a change.

When I believe its okay not to do something the same way every time:

- I take more chances.
- I accept alternatives I never considered before
- I become more comfortable with uncertainty

And it becomes okay to miss the turn.

Nip/Tuck's Life Coach

The television show Nip/Tuck (drama about plastic surgeons in Miami) featured a life coach, Ava. She was hired to help out Julia, the wife of one of the doctors. After Julia saw some success, she hired Ava to work with her son Matt. Matt was having trouble keeping good grades in school. So Ava agreed if Matt achieved a certain grade she would have sex with him. With this incentive, Matt indeed achieved the grade. Not only did Ava have sex with him, she started to date this 17 year old boy. This upset her 16 year old son greatly because now his mom wasn't having sex with him. It turns out he was only her adopted son since she had once been a man and physically couldn't have children of her own.

When I first saw this I thought this could be bad press for coaches! But then I laughed – one of the writers clearly must have had a bad experience with a coach!

But what an advertisement. And what carte blanche it gives me!

I mean, no matter how radical I am with one of my clients, within our sessions or with assignments, it can't possibly come close to the over-the-top depiction of a coach on this TV show! Trust me, I'm creative and innovative with challenges and exercises, but not quite like Ava!

This is a great example of how I can perceive something. I can look at this as an insult and have the feelings that follow when I think in this way.

Or, I can look at this as an example of a coach going over-the-top! I can ignore it, or use it when I talk to prospective clients.

When I don't limit myself to seeing the negativity of a situation:

- I can laugh
- I can be creative
- I can be motivated and get into action

Here's to more outrageous coaches on television dramas! It's free publicity!

Not What I Imagined for My Vacation

I had strained my calf but flew cross country to celebrate my dad's birthday. I didn't give my sprained calf as much attention as it deserved the week between the strain and getting on the plane.

Turns out, I had pulled a muscle in my calf.

A friend stated the obvious: *this injury is going to ruin your vacation!*

By the time I got to my destination, I was in a lot more pain due to walking through the airports. I could barely stand.

The original plan was to visit my parents then go spend some time with my friend.

But because of the pain, I had to rethink what I was going to do for the week.

I couldn't go bike riding.
I couldn't play tennis.
There was only so far I could walk with my crutches.

What I <u>could</u> do was take my pain medicine, sleep a lot, and swim a little.

I decided to stay at my parents. I mean, the pool was handicapped accessible making it easy for me to maneuver into the water.

I could have gotten really upset at the change of plans. And maybe I would have fought having to change the plans if the pain wasn't as intense as it was.

But for whatever reason, I accepted the change.

And it was what it was.

There could have been zillions of undesirable places to stay when I was recuperating. Instead I had great weather, an enclosed deck to enjoy, and parents who helped but also left me alone.

When I accept changes I wasn't expecting:

- I'm not fighting what I can't control.
- I can enjoy or at least appreciate what I have
- I don't waste my time

This doesn't mean we have to settle for something we don't want. But, when there are circumstances we can't fight, accepting them can be so much easier.

Nothing Is Free

Someone had told me about a service where you could download music for free. I was surprised this existed after the Napster legal decisions a few years ago.

Since I hadn't tried this back then, I downloaded this software onto my computer.

There was so much music you could download!

Classic rock, the 70's, show tunes, rare rhythm and blue. Even Lulu!! (*To Sir, With Love*).

At first it was great to hear some of this music again. *Stairway to Heaven, One in a Million You, Break it to Me Gently.*

It made me think of other songs I wanted to download. It made me think of how I should organize this music on my computer. It made me think I should go through ALL my cassette tapes, see which ones I wanted to find online so I could download them and listen to them on my computer. It made me want to research Billboards hits in the 70's and 80's to see if there were any I had never owned yet wanted to download now.

It made me stop and realize what I was doing!

All told I had spent about five hours downloading the music. With the projects I was thinking of I easily added another 20 hours of downloading music.

This is not how I want to spend my life!

I have goals in my life and when I want to chill out there are many, many other activities to do besides sitting by my computer alone downloading music.

For me, downloading music is not free. It costs me time and disconnection from others, myself, and what I am passionate about.

When I stopped an activity I initially thought of as exciting and realized it was getting obsessive:

- I felt more myself
- I was more relaxed
- I was more alive

If I really want this music, I can buy it or see if a friend has it. As a result, the music software is no longer on my computer. I guess I'll have to do without the Bertie Higgins recording of *Key Largo*.

Only One Way to Go from Here

When I teach my management and leadership classes the attendees fill out evaluation forms. They give feedback on the course, the location and on me.

Generally, I get very good results.

One time I even got a perfect score.

Someone from the company where I contracted to do the training called me to congratulate me, she was thrilled.

It was nice to get this call and get the recognition.

But there really is only one way to go from here.

In contrast, I played in a tennis match where my partner and I were destroyed. We won a few games but pretty much couldn't do much worse than we did.

But there really is only one way to go from here.

In fact, there have been subsequent courses where the evals have gone down a bit.

And there have been matches where we have won.

But I have been able to enjoy all these moments, whether winning or losing, or getting a perfect score.

I wouldn't have always enjoyed them.

In my early years as an instructor, I would have focused on the imperfections. I wouldn't have seen the wisdom of losing.

Am I wiser because I'm older?

I hope not!

I believe it is about focus and passion.

When I am focused and passionate about what I'm doing:

- It's about the process not the result
- The challenges are shifted to opportunities
- I appreciate when things go well because I know what it's like when they don't!

As long as I keep this perspective, there really isn't only one way to go when you've achieved perfection or total disaster. Rather, there are a myriad of alternatives which you seamlessly flow between.

Oops!

I got to my softball game about five minutes after our call time. As I got onto the field, I saw no one from my team. I thought this was strange since I was running late.

Turns out I wasn't five minutes late.

I was two hours and five minutes late.

I had missed the entire game.

Oops.

I screwed up on the time – I confused it with the practice time for the day before (a practice I couldn't attend).

In over 10 years of softball I had never done this before.

I felt bad and hoped there had been enough players to field a team (turns out they had just enough).

But mostly I laughed about it.

What else could I do?

I suppose I could intently examine why this happens, the hidden reasons why I really didn't want to play softball, or how I need to be more focused in my life or whatever.

Or I could chalk it up to being just one of those things.

I owned the mistake and contacted the manager as soon as I was able.

Then I made sure I was on time for my next event!

When I own mistakes I make:

- I show I'm human
- I don't have to be defensive
- I alleviate conflict

I'm human. I'll continue to make mistakes. But admitting them isn't one of those mistakes.

Opening a Power Bar

I have trouble opening up a power bar. You know, those bars you eat when you want a burst of energy.

The packages don't tear apart easily. So, I get impatient and try to rip the wrapping with my teeth. But this doesn't seem to work either. It gets frustrating since I'm usually trying to open it while I'm in action – either driving, at the gym or on my bike.

I was at the gym, and I was having this particular trouble. I happened to take a moment to glance down at the power bar. Right on the wrapper it said

To Open: Hold Here. Lift and Tear

I held there. I lifted, and it tore.

It was simple and easy to do.

Funny how this happens when you follow instructions!

How often have I ended up taking more time and getting more frustrated because I didn't take a moment to follow instructions?

Either my impatience, thinking I don't need instructions, or willfulness can sometimes cause me to take five steps for something which should take only one.

Where in my life am I not following instructions?

Instructions are information and advice. They are there to help. Isn't it nice to get help and support?

When I follow instructions:

- I feel accomplished
- I have direction
- Life is easier

Following instructions doesn't mean following the herd or not thinking for yourself. It means taking a moment to stay focused on what we want to accomplish.

So *hold*, *lift* and *tear* as often as possible.

Open to the Unexpected

Whenever I have a birthday celebration for myself, I foot the bill for my guests. This could mean a dinner out, but more likely, a celebration at my house or friend's house where I create the main course and everyone else can bring side dishes or something to drink if they choose.

I don't feel comfortable inviting people to go to a restaurant and expecting them to pay. Besides, it's usually noisy and the table is in a rectangle so you really can't speak to everyone.

So you can imagine my feelings when I'm invited to someone else's party where it's a dinner at a restaurant.

Recently a good friend was celebrating his 40th birthday and invited us all to a Moroccan restaurant.

While I was thrilled to be celebrating with him, I wasn't happy about the circumstances. But since I decided to go, I decided to go with a good attitude, and I'm happy to say as I was heading to the restaurant I was in a good mind set.

As soon as I walked into the restaurant, my whole being shifted.

It wasn't just a restaurant -- rather it didn't look like a restaurant -- it looked like something you'd find, well, in Morocco!

We weren't seated at a table -- the place was filled with couches with tables around them.

I knew I was in for a special treat.

The evening was filled with lots of conversation, good wine, belly dancing, and a five course meal.

When the bill came, and I had to pay my portion I thought to myself

Is that all?!

I also glanced at the time, as I was leaving. I had arrived at 7 p.m., and it was now almost 11!

The meal ended up being a four hour celebratory event!

If I had stayed in a mind set about how one should celebrate one's birthday, I may not have gone to the event or had been open to how fantastic it could be. Fortunately this didn't happen.

Where else in my life do I stay shut off to the unexpected? What would I be missing?

When I am open to the unexpected:

- I accept challenges
- I expand my way of thinking
- I'm living life larger

Being open to the unexpected allows me to take in – everything!

Penny Wise, Pound Foolish

I was working with a business partner. While the hourly rate was attractive, there was no payment for prep work.

My role required a lot of prep.

This decreased my hourly rate significantly, way below my required minimum and sometimes low enough that working at a fast food restaurant flipping burgers might have been more lucrative.

I was being *penny wise and pound foolish.*

I rationalized business would pick up and my prep would decrease however this wasn't happening, and while it could happen, it wasn't in the foreseeable future.

Yet I stayed working in this situation for several additional months.

Why?

Quite simply - ***fear.***

If I gave the job up, how would I replace the revenue stream? Albeit the pay was low but it was money.

How ironic, I coach people to move past their fears. I do this precise work with them and see the incredible breakthroughs and results they get. Yet, I couldn't do the same myself in this case.

The fear was driving me so strongly it made my penny wise and pound foolish belief more powerful.

Until I admitted it.

Until I started talking about it.

Until I laughed about it.

Then I let it go.

I gave up this business opportunity.

When fear drives me and I am being penny wise and pound foolish:

- I shut myself from other opportunities I wouldn't have time to notice
- My quality of life suffers
- I'm not focused on what I want to do

Fear stops us from living life. When we admit we are afraid, we can begin releasing it and take action. The fear then stops driving us.

Planning vs. Worrying

I was going on a retreat in Southern California. I decided I wanted to camp outside instead of staying in the dormitory style rooms. Also, since I was flying down I wanted to minimize what to bring on the plane with me.

I was going to my brother's the day before the retreat. I thought he had a tent but wanted to confirm this with him. After asking him I also inquired if I could borrow a couple of pillows.

His response was yes but also

"You seem to be worrying about this a lot."

Button pushed.

I got pretty defensive and replied
"I'm not worried I'm planning."

His response

"That's something Mom would say, but you would say she was worrying."

Another button pushed.

Conversation over.

I wasn't worrying; I was planning, so I could be organized.

But, I started wondering about the difference between planning and worrying?

Actually in those moments, I wasn't *wondering* what the difference was I was *worrying* about it!

The thought process made me realize that *worrying* was about being stuck in a moment, in a cycle with no out.

Planning was proactive and freeing.

Sure, too much *planning* could be confining and compulsive.

But, when I'm *planning* instead of *worrying*:

- I'm attune to the present
- I'm not coming from fear but instead, looking for results
- I have the choice to worry about something else

So now I'll plan how not to let my brother push my buttons.

Playing Softball in the Rain

In my eighth year of playing softball I started questioning whether I wanted to put in the time to continue with the season. I decided to take it one weekend at a time and see what happened.

The weekend after this decision the weather was not great. It was a little cool and it seemed like it might rain. Our game wasn't scheduled until later in the afternoon, so it was possible the rain would pick up, and our game would be cancelled.

This didn't happen, and we needed to play.

In the middle of the game, it started to rain. Not enough to call the game, but enough to be a distraction.

I loved it!

Having to field the ball as well as hit and then run the bases while it was raining was a new experience. Instead of being aggravated, I was laughing! It was what I needed to bring back some lost energy and passion about the game.

I did worry about future games – what would it take next to keep me interested – flying bullets?

But the experience was enough to give me the energy I needed to continue throughout the season.

An outside circumstance affected an activity I had been doing for years. I embraced this circumstance, and my vigor for softball was renewed.
When I allow myself to accept new ways to do things which have become ritual:

- It brings a new perspective to the activity
- It brings a renewed excitement and passion
- It energizes me in all areas of my life

Preventive Not Preventative

The word <u>preventive</u> is a common word. And, for most of my life I pronounced it as *preventative*. It wasn't until I started working with Blue Cross Blue Shield and comparing diagnostic to preventive diagnosis that I realized (rather I was told) there was only one pronunciation: <u>preventive</u> not *preventative*.

How could this be? Well, it was a very East Coast thing to say it the wrong way. We all said it wrong, so it wasn't noticed.

I was talking to my brother.; my niece wasn't feeling well, and I suggested a homeopathic medicine we all take. *Good idea* he said. *It's preventative*.

I laughed and told him there was no such pronunciation. He didn't believe it and went to verify if *preventative* was a correct pronunciation by asking his wife. She agreed with him.

Not a surprise, she grew up in the same area where we grew up.

My brother could have asked his friends, our parents, former teachers and the majority probably would have pronounced the word as *preventative*, not <u>preventive</u>.

He went to the dictionary. The word *preventative* was there – the phonetics had you say it as <u>preventive</u>, and the definition referred to <u>preventive</u>.

Oh.

My brother didn't want to accept the correct pronunciation of this word. Well, neither did I when I first heard this.

It's difficult to accept something being different than you always thought it was.

But where does this limit us?

Where in my life have I seen things one way, only to discover so many other opportunities if I could see it differently?

I do like knowing lights will come on when I flip the switch, and I'll get a dial tone when I pick up the phone. It's comforting to be certain of things.

But when I'm able to accept things could be different than the ways I've always thought them to me:

- I'm open to more opportunities
- I realize learning is infinite
- Uncomfortable things are a little easier to handle

And it's easier to pronounce <u>preventive</u> correctly.

Preventive vs. Preventative PART TWO

Some time ago I wrote a piece about the fact that there is no such word as *preventative*. I explained that I learned this while contracting with a health benefits company. I "proved" it by looking in one dictionary where phonetically it was pronounced *preventive* not *preventative*.

Since my brother was one of the people to whom I subsequently taught this lesson, he took it to heart.

One day he explained this to someone he knew. This guy proved my brother wrong.

I looked at the evidence my brother presented (I should mention, my brother is a lawyer) and emailed the trainer who taught me, to show her the word *preventative* does in fact exist.

Her response: *Yep…the word has always existed. It's just that "preventive" is the preferred word.*

But this can't be! I have a published story which says *preventative* doesn't exist. I will have to delete this story from my 2nd edition.

My brother reminded me, this is what my book is about: shifting difficult situations to opportunities.

What's difficult about this is that it's very embarrassing to have something wrong in written proof. The opportunity is that I don't have to hide this or be embarrassed. I am able to admit I was mistaken.

I obviously heard what I wanted to hear when I learned this the first time and jumped to a conclusion, which I put in writing!

When I admit my mistakes:

- I have the opportunity to see how I can learn from wrong conclusions
- I change my focus to see things differently
- My embarrassment is released

Included in the email from my trainer was this:

*Even though <u>preventive</u> is preferred, and that's what we want to teach people to use, the language might be changing, and one day <u>preventative</u> will be the preferred usage. My English teacher friends are always reminding me language **shifts**...and that's why we don't say shan't anymore!*

So not only can we shift difficult situations to opportunities, but the vocabulary we use will shift as well!

Problems with the Valet

I was on a training assignment where all expenses were paid. At the hotel I didn't park my own car; I left it with the valet.

I had developed a habit of calling downstairs before I wanted the car so it would be ready for me when I got there.

On one of my days off, I called downstairs only to find the line was busy. I called several times, and kept getting a busy signal.

Finally, I got through, but the phone kept ringing and ringing and ringing.

I got irritated. I got aggravated. I got angry. I started laughing.

What kind of life do I lead where I'm having trouble with getting my car from the valet?

Here I was on a training project which paid well and was energetic, fun, and exciting, and I was getting aggravated because I can't go, or rather I chose not to go and get my own car.

This realization put things into perspective for me. I didn't beat myself up for getting *irritated, aggravated, and angry.* But, I accepted how I felt and how ridiculous it was – I became grateful for being able to be *irritated, aggravated and angry* over something so trivial. After all, why should I expect to be so privileged.

When I can put things in perspective:

- I switch from negative thoughts to optimism
- I recognize what is really important
- I laugh at what is petty

Of course, if the maids don't clean my room when I want them to, it's a whole different story.

Respecting Time

Like many other kids in their teens, I had braces. I hated going to the orthodontist's office because a five minute checkup would take two hours, most of it sitting in the reception area. The doctor overbooked himself, so I often sat around waiting even though my appointment time would come and go.

I mentioned this one night at dinner and my father didn't believe this was happening. He decided to come with me to one of my appointments. We got to the doctor's office a few moments before our scheduled time. Sure enough my time came and went.

When fifteen minutes went by, my dad went up to the receptionist desk to see when I would have my appointment. He didn't get a definite answer.

Thirty minutes past my scheduled appointment time my dad went back to the receptionist. She explained it was normal for the kids to wait since the mothers usually left their kids while they did their shopping!

My dad demanded to see the orthodontist. He said one thing to the doctor.

I respect your time; please respect mine.

Much to the horror of the reception staff, I was escorted right in. Not only that, but every appointment following I was taken in at my scheduled time.

This lesson stays with me as an adult. I still understand what being on time means. I'm not always on time (ask some of my friends) but I do try to be on time or let people know when I'm running late.

As a coach I notice that when my clients aren't on time, they also aren't focused, energetic or fully alive. When they are on time, we get into action a lot more easily.

There are only 24 hours in a day no matter who we are. If I schedule time with others and with myself and I respect those times I end up being:

- More accomplished
- More present
- More content

Respecting the time of others starts by managing my own time. This means trimming or revitalizing my schedule. Then it's easier to respect the value of other people's time and to focus on what's happening, rather then be in a mode of catching up.

This is more peaceful and what I deserve.

Rushing to Yoga

A client meeting went over schedule, and I had 15 minutes to get to yoga. I jumped into my car and impatiently drove behind a city bus until I could pull around. With eight minutes left, I had trouble finding parking. I found a spot only to realize it was street cleaning day. I saw another spot which I managed to get by cutting across the street and backing into it although I had to wait a few moments to let a bike rider pass.

I parked the car and ran furiously to the gym. I threw my bag into a locker and managed to get to the class in time to breathe and get centered.

The irony of the situation didn't escape me.

But I allowed myself to focus on my adrenaline rush as I was in pursuit to get to a place where I would become centered.

I guess at times I like the contrast of feeling frazzled and then being centered. I enjoyed the rushed feeling. I enjoyed the obstacles I came upon.

It's not always my goal to feel peaceful. A level of stress and anxiety is good for me.

When I accept this:

- I don't fight my feelings so the stress and anxiety works with me, not against me.
- I'm right there and present
- My levels of peace and stress flow more seamlessly together.

I believe success comes more easily when I welcome anxiety and stress, rather than fight it. It gives energy like yoga gives energy.

These are different energies, but both are needed in my life.

Saying Goodbye

I remember an episode from the original Star Trek where Dr. Spock was stranded in a different time and place with a woman with whom he fell in love. He either could spend the rest of his life "stuck" in this place or rejoin life.

In one moment, he held her hand and her gaze. In a flash, he was a million miles and years away.

Dramatic? Yes!!

But to me saying goodbye can sometimes be intense.

I remember when my grandma would say goodbye to her friends. They said goodbye as if it would be the last time they would see each other.

I remember when I moved cross country and said goodbye to my parents, not knowing when I would see them again – it turned out to only be a few weeks later.

But, I still don't like goodbyes–not with my parents or good friends.

I don't like goodbyes because these people make me feel like I'm home.

It's also my desire to have those I love around me.

Instead of focusing on how these people aren't with me always, I acknowledge that there are so many people in my life I wish I could be with always.

When I acknowledge this:

- I realize these people are always around one way or another
- I feel supported
- I feel like the luckiest person in the world!

Shuttle or Taxi

I was attending a conference. I had taken our train system (BART) to my destination. I called the hotel where the conference was being held to find out if they had a shuttle which could take me to my meeting.

The shuttle would arrive in five or ten minutes. Or I could walk across the street and take a taxi for $10.

Without hesitation, I took the taxi.

Why?

I had had surgery a few days before this meeting. The surgery was on my left hand (and I'm a lefty!)

While I was well enough to attend the meeting I still was in pain.

I didn't want to wait to get to the meeting.

I was in complete acceptance of where I was physically.

There were times I would have fought my current physical condition.

I would have thought:

If I were well, I would have driven

If I were well, I wouldn't be spending the money

If I were well, I would wait

Instead, I took care of myself in the moment.

When I'm in acceptance:

- I moved towards solutions more thoroughly.
- I don't waste time with *what ifs*

- I experience fewer conflicts and more peace. I can take action.

While I can't wait to be fully functioning again, I am grateful. I'm accepting the physical limitations I have at the moment, so I can still experience everything I can in the present.

Staying Dry or Playing in the Rain?

One particularly rainy day when my niece was only two years old her dad (my brother) got her excited about bundling up, going out and playing in the rain. She even wanted to bring a bar of soap so she could bathe!

How many adults want to play in the rain? Where would our optimism be if we did see the value in getting wet?

As I was leaving the gym on a rainy day, someone who was leaving at the same time asked me if I was keeping dry.

I blurted out "I don't care!"

I don't know where this answer came from!

It wasn't rude (at least that wasn't my intent) or sarcastic.

It was more a statement of acceptance, at least in the moment.

I didn't care about staying dry.

Let it rain. I'll get wet, so what, I can dry off later!

There was a sense of freedom in saying it and meaning it.

How many times have I hesitated or tried to find a reason not to go out because it was raining, using not wanting to get wet as an excuse.

When I truly don't care if I stay dry in inclement weather:

- My attitude is coming from within. I'm not letting outside forces influence me.
- I'm open to adventure
- I can see things which were obstacles as opportunities

And I'm more optimistic despite the weather!

Staying True to the Moment

During one softball game, I was playing left field and a pop up came towards me. I ran to the ball and made the catch. Since there was a guy on first base I got ready to throw the ball to my cut off so the guy didn't tag up to second. However, as I went to throw the ball, I dropped it. I calmly picked it up and proceeded to throw it in.

What had happened, without my knowledge, is the guy on first wasn't going to run but when he saw me drop the ball, he took it as an opportunity to tag up. Because I continued to throw the ball in we put the runner out. My error helped us get a double play!

I'd like to say I planned the whole thing; it was my clever and creative mind at work. Besides the fact no one would believe it, it isn't true. It's also probable if I planned something like that it would backfire.

What really happened was I was in the moment. I stayed true to the moment. I made a mistake, but I followed through with my actions. This was done without premeditated thought; it was instinct.

By staying true to the moment I was able to:

- Stay right where I was
- Follow through
- Have faith in my actions.

Wouldn't it be great if I could stay in the moment *all the time*?

Not realistic.

But being in the moment is a gift and I welcome more gifts.

Stretching

I had recovered from an injury to the point where it wasn't obvious to anyone that I had had one. But, if I wanted to continue to be as physically active as I always was, I would need to continue to stretch.

Everyday.

Forever.

This was daunting to me. While I had stretched more in the last few years, obviously it hadn't been enough. And, to avoid re-injury or new injuries, more frequent stretching would be required, even on days when I wasn't playing softball, bike riding, hiking or playing tennis.

I could consider myself very lucky to have gone so far in my life being lazy about stretching.

But it's still not fair! Why can't I still be lazy, stretch only a little and do what I do? I'm already too busy, now I have to add yet more time for stretching.

So with this not so great attitude I started to think about stretching more metaphorically.

Not only do I need to physically stretch my body every day, but I also need to stretch in all areas of my life.

With business, friends, interests and hobbies.

Without stretching I become complacent. I'm not growing; I'm drifting in my life.

When I stretch myself in every way:

- I can't live more in the moment then I am right then
- I push myself past fear to opportunity
- What was uncomfortable is now comfortable

Essentially stretching *me* every day isn't a big deal – it only benefits *my life*.

So I'm thinking I don't need to stretch myself every day.

I want to.

Except when I don't.

Oh well that's the way it goes sometimes.

Stuck in the Elevator

I met with one of my clients in the late afternoon.

She was very relaxed, calm and focused. There were times in the past where she was more scattered.

Earlier that day she had gone to one of her clients for a meeting. She was going up the ancient elevator to the office when the elevator got stuck.

She was stuck in an old unstable elevator alone and without a button to push to get help.

She did have her cell phone and managed, after calling repeatedly, to get someone from the office.

They managed to get the elevator moving after some time (apparently this was not the first time the elevator got stuck).

But, being stuck in the elevator forced my client to stop. It made her think about what was important.

This resulted in not stressing over things which normally bother her.

How interesting that it took getting stuck in the elevator to slow down.

But, it makes sense. It forced her to stop.

There is so much value in stopping.

I was forced to stop when I had an accident and broke my leg. Others are forced to stop when they are confronted with illness, trauma, or death.

Why can't we stop just to stop?

When we stop:

- We get the chance to simply "be."
- We breathe throughout our body.
- We see what's important in our lives.

Breathing exercises, meditation, yoga, massage, acupuncture.

They all help me to stop.

When I stop, I'm given the perspective to go again.

Swinging at the Ball

I've been playing softball a long time now. My involvement, relationship, passion and connection with the game have had their ups and downs over the years.

I have tried different things to keep the energy high, sometimes it's worked, sometimes not.

Recently, I was playing and was up to bat. It was my second time at the plate.

The first time I walked.

I knew this would most likely be my last time at bat.

I didn't want to walk again; I wanted to hit the ball.

I had a full count (3 balls, 2 strikes) on me.

The pitch came.

I swung and fouled out (in softball, a foul ball counts as strike three).

I was out.

It could be justified that I swung to protect the plate.

But it took me a little while to admit this to myself.

I knew the pitch was a ball.

My desire to hit the ball was stronger than my desire to walk yet again.

I was being completely selfish.

To the outside world, it could look like I was protecting the plate.

But, I've been in this situation before, and I didn't swing. I have been under the pressure of a full count and took the pitch and walked. It is very rare I would take a pitch on full count which was a strike.

Plain and simple I did what some of my clients have done when they're building their businesses to the success they want. Everything is working out, and all of a sudden they aren't needed as much.

They sabotage themselves.

While the situation is different, this is what I did.

For whatever reason, the pitcher was having difficulty throwing strikes to me. I should have accepted this and taken the walks.

But internally, I wasn't feeling valued by only walking and not hitting the balls. I sacrificed the team's well being and success for this selfishness.

While I don't believe we would have caught up to win the game, it is possible we would have gotten more runs if I had taken the walk. I was the third out. Walking would have meant I got on base and another batter would have had a chance.

We'll never know.

But when I take an action for the sake of being in motion rather than for a valued purpose:

- I could be going against the flow in a negative way
- I create chaos or a negative outcome
- The result is most likely not what I wanted

Sometimes standing there and taking the walk is the best hit you can make.

Taking for Granted Something Which Was Once Difficult

I volunteered at a fundraiser where I sold raffle tickets as one of Santa's helpers, dressed only in Santa pants and a hat.

This was the second year I had done this.

The first year I was nervous about doing the event. The insecurity came from the perceived reactions I would get from others.

I didn't think of any of those things this year.

What was once a barrier for me was something I now took for granted. Something I didn't even think about.

But, it does deserve to be thought about. It deserves acknowledgement and accomplishment.

How many times do we achieve a goal and not celebrate the achievement?

We think it's not big enough for recognition, its no big deal.

But, what if we celebrated all accomplishments, large or small? How would that change interactions between all of us?

When I don't take things for granted but take time to celebrate my accomplishments, no matter how trivial I think they are:

- I am honoring myself
- I can recognize other people's achievements
- I am grateful

How can I know how far I've come if I don't look back and appreciate the path I've taken, the conflicts I've learned from, and the success I've achieved?

The results of this reflection can only lead to more success!

Tennis

In the last couple of years I've been playing more tennis. I'm not a beginner but I'm also not advanced – I'd call myself an intermediate advanced beginner. But I enjoy the game.

I have one friend whose level of play and mine are pretty equal. However, I had hand surgery, which put me off the tennis courts for about two months. In this interim, he had started taking lessons.

I knew this could put me at a serious disadvantage (we are both healthily competitive about our games!)

The first time I played something bizarre happened –

I never played better.

It was doubles, which was different for me. But I learned what it meant to play the net, and I was able to return serves I never could return before.

I was amazed and excited.

Some days later it was time for the singles match. My friend (I wouldn't be so crass to mention his name) joked that he would whoop me.

We played, and to my surprise, it was close.

And the further surprise – I won!

After taking time off for surgery on my left hand (and I'm left handed)—and learning that all the while Tom (oops) was taking lessons–I was thrilled to win!

How?

Whether he believes it or not, Tom set it up for me to win. He created a condition where I was comfortable and relaxed.

In the 1970's Tim Gallwey wrote a book called *The Inner Game of Tennis*. In it he emphasizes how the mind is as important to the game as the actual play.

With Tom's declaration of his intent to whoop me, he set me up to win. He did this because:

- The circumstances of surgery and time made it seem obvious I wouldn't win
- I had nothing to lose by playing
- If I won a few games, his declaration would be false.

Indeed when I won three games I felt victorious. The rest was gravy.

My inner game works favorably with me when:

- I don't have set expectations
- I stay focused right in the moment
- I can reset goals which don't turn out exactly as planned by seeing them as accomplishments

Since this first set, Tom and I have played several more sets.

I have won every time. The games and sets are incredibly close. Our last set went overtime to 10-8 games.

Yes, there is a thrill with my wins.

But, the real win is that we are both improving, and each game is more challenging and exciting, resulting in a tremendous high!

And winning is a little extra fun!

The Chill Factor

My shower is quirky - every time I turn it on, it first puts out cold water for a brief moment before the temperature gets to the setting of what I want.

So I've gotten into the habit of standing out of the way for the first second or two when I turn on the shower.

That is until I wasn't able to stand in the shower due to an injury. I had to use shower seat and was sitting directly in the line of the water's fire.

The cold water.

At first I dreaded this and tried to think of ways to avoid this cold blast. Finally I realized I had no choice but to deal with the cold.

By the third of fourth time, I had gotten into a routine. I would count to three, take a deep breath, and turn the water on. The cold water would pour on me and, fortunately turn warm pretty quickly.

I started to enjoy this process and, in fact, laughed through the ritual. I was now laughing about something I had initially dreaded.

When I laugh through situations I first dreaded:

- They aren't as bad as they originally appeared
- I can feel anticipation and excitement instead of the dread
- I don't get bogged down in details which really aren't important

This doesn't mean I'm not going to move out of the way of the cold water when I'm back to standing in the shower.

Or does it?

Howard Miller

The Joke About the Snail

There is an old joke:

A man hears his doorbell ring, and he goes to answer the door. At the door is a snail who says "Hi how are you?"

The guy kicks the snail over to the next house and closes the door.

A year later the doorbell rings again and the guy goes to answer the door. When he opens the door the same snail is there and says "why you'd do that for?!"

Funny joke on the surface.

I then thought more about it. This snail, while persistent, spent a year in anger and confusion to get an answer to his question (and hopefully wasn't kicked to the next house again!)

How much time do I spend in anger and confusion?

If I added all the times I do that, would it add up to a year in my life? More? How much more?!

Ugh! I don't really want to calculate that –

I only know that I'd rather hope, from this point on, that the time I spend in *gratitude, joy, laughing,* and *keeping it simple* far outweighs the time I spend pondering what I did wrong or why I don't have what others have.

Focusing on this hope:

- Keeps me optimistic
- Keeps me laughing
- Keeps me keeping it simple!

The Pity Party

One of my clients is an executive who is always at odds with his board of directors. He feels they don't do enough so, of course, as a result, they never live up to his expectations.

The reason he feels this way involves a history of actions between him and the board over the last several years.

But more than half of the original board has changed throughout this time!

This awareness made my client realize he was only hurting himself with these thoughts. It placed him into his *pity party*.

He is making tremendous conscious efforts to stay out of his *pity party* and look at the board differently.

He has made great progress but like anything else, there are ups and downs.

Recently, I asked him how he was doing. He said:

"I was in my pity party. But I didn't go to the VIP lounge this time!"

I loved the comment.

I know I have my pity parties. They can last only a moment or span over some days. And while we might rationalize that if we're going to have the party, we might as well make it splashy, if we indulge in the party too often and have made it too comfortable - *we're stuck.*

Then, the VIP lounge is not just splashy but an excuse to stay in our negativity.

Pity parties... Feeling sorry for ourselves...

It's human.

But when I recognize I'm at the party too long:

- I think of something I could be appreciative or grateful for – and pretend to be until I actually am
- I do something – anything – even smile – which is different than what I was doing
- I get over being bored because staying in those feelings is boring.

Occasionally I go to parties where I do go to the VIP lounge. But those parties have room for more than one living creature.

The Poker Game

For about a decade, I've been getting together with a group of friends for a regular poker game. It's social and friendly, but we do play for money. I always have the attitude of being prepared to lose $60. (We play quarter – half dollar – dollar stakes). This way if I do lose, I'm okay with it and see it as spending money on a nice night out.

While I do win more than lose, I always wonder how I can improve my game, strategies, or techniques before and during the game.

This one particular game, I hadn't prepared or thought about strategizing much. I started winning from the first or second hand and continued to win throughout the evening. The cards (and the chips) kept coming to me. Every possible win became a reality. There was nothing I could do except win! I won over $100.

Why did this happen?

I really have no idea. It just did. It was effortless. I didn't make smart plays or bad moves I was only present to what was happening.

And I won.

Sometimes planning, strategy or preparing doesn't matter. Sometimes its luck and being in the moment.

When you recognize that luck and being in the moment can change a situation:

- You are more open to risk
- You realize you can't control everything despite any preparations you have made
- You are grateful when luck is on your side!

And enjoy it as long as it lasts. Because it will end – until it comes back again!

The Tomato at My Door

I was out of town for a training contract. It was a productive yet tiring week. By the end of the week I wanted to have a somewhat mellow evening - go to the gym and bring in some dinner.

As I was heading out to the gym, I bumped into some co-workers from the project. For some reason I mentioned I wanted a tomato in the morning. The hotel's breakfast of eggs, bacon, and muffins was getting to me; I needed my healthy regimen back!

The person in charge of the project thought for a moment and realized she had a home grown heirloom tomato in her room! Would I like to have it?

I did, but I really didn't want to go to her room to get it, nor did I want her to have to go up to her room and bring it downstairs. So I thanked her and told her I would get something at the supermarket.

An hour or so later I got back.

There on the door handle to my hotel room was an heirloom tomato!

She had gone back to her room and brought it to my door.

The action made me smile immediately! It was a kind, thoughtful and generous thing to do.

This woman was running the project. Yet, she took time to give this gift filled with generosity.

Maybe the giving was a gift to her as well?

How do I feel when I do something *selfless* for someone else?

When I am *selfless* in my actions:

- I step out of any stress I might be in
- I'm not focused entirely on me
- I smile!

Being *selfless* doesn't require huge sacrifices. It can be a simple act which lifts the spirits of someone else.

Imagine how *less stressful* the world would be if we all were a little more *selfless*.

The Youngest Sings the Four Questions

In a Passover Seder, which celebrates freedom, there is a tradition where the youngest member at the table would ask the four questions about the holiday. One could also sing these questions.

When I was a child I would sing the four questions.

There would always be a younger member at the table, but since most people don't sing the questions, I would always be asked to sing them.

Eventually, I didn't want to be assigned this task associated with children. But, the adults would always want me to do it.

I resented this.

As I became an adult and spent more Seders with adults, family, and non family, I would end up being the only person who could sing these questions.

At first it was embarrassing and tedious for me. Can't anyone else do this? Why do I have to?

Now I'm at a point in my life where I welcome singing the four questions. I offer, when appropriate. I hope I can be 80 and sing the four questions.

When I stopped fighting it:

- It's a freeing feeling
- It bonds me to my past and to my future
- I cherish it

How many other things in my life have I looked at with embarrassment instead of accomplishment? Where has this stopped me from getting all I want and yes, all I deserve?

That's a question I don't sing at a Passover Seder, but one I think about to help me get all I want and deserve.

Theories Which Change in a Second

Years ago, I decided I wouldn't buy any property until I was in a relationship.

Then one day, while on vacation, a voice came into my head which said:

What does one thing have to do with the other?

When I returned home I started looking for property and three weeks later, despite the heavy competition, I had my first piece of property.

Now I can beat myself up for not having that thought years before (and I sometimes go there, although it does no good!) or I can analyze why I had the theory to begin with, but it doesn't matter.

I can also try to figure out why I had this thought on vacation, but it doesn't matter either.

I'm only grateful it surfaced to my consciousness, and I acted on it

My original theory kept me stuck. I didn't know it until I questioned it.

How many other theories do I have in my life? How do they serve me or keep me stuck?

I have looked at many of those and as a result, have made changes, large and small, to my life. I've changed everything from what I do for a living to what I watch on TV.

When I have the clarity to look at my thoughts and theories and determine how they serve me:

- I am not staying stagnate or stuck
- I am allowing variety to come into my life
- I'm creating a powerful future

They're All Staring at Me. Oh, They Aren't

I was visiting my parents in Florida. They live in one of those complexes where everyone who is still alive from their childhood, their younger adult years, old neighbors, old teachers of mine, and friend and relatives of all of the above live as well. They also get to meet all the people they somehow didn't meet in the last 70 years.

I wanted to go to the gym while I was there and once again my parents mentioned the gym on the premises. I usually go to a gym near them, but not the one in the compound.

This trip I decided I would try their gym.

It wasn't a full gym, but adequate for a workout.

The biggest difference, to me, was everyone there was 20 to 40 years older than I am!

I immediately felt uncomfortable – what was I doing there? They will watch my every move.

But rather than bolt, I decided to proceed with my workout.

I became less self-conscious the longer I was there.

I also realized that everyone else was doing his or her own thing.

There were no prolonged stares or whispers about me.

Was I relieved or disappointed?

I'm sure I was noticed because I was younger – and how often does this NOT HAPPEN in my life?

But my self consciousness came about because I thought I was "more" than I was in the situation

When I relaxed and realized *it wasn't about me*:

- I could do what I came there to do
- I could relax
- I could laugh at how my swelled importance of myself can get in the way

If I concern myself with other's reactions, or the awkwardness I feel in a situation, then I feel awkward. When I focus on what I set out to do, it'll happen.

This Isn't SO Bad!

There are times when I focus on how I'm not growing my business fast enough.

When I take on this focus, it raises my stress level. When my stress level is raised, it brings a new intensity to my worrying. Then, my stress goes even higher. Then, I worry about the stress.

And so it goes.

One particular day I had this focus on my business when I didn't have a lot of time. I needed to meet my workout partner at the gym, but I also had to wait until the housekeeper arrived. I was hoping he'd arrive early so I'd have time to get to my condo to pick up my tenant's rent check.

It wasn't until after my workout and I was sitting in a café with my wireless connection hooked up on my laptop that I started laughing.

How bad could it be if I were meeting my workout partner in the middle of the day? And had a housekeeper? And a condo?

Isn't one of the attractions of having my own business to be able to set my own hours, giving me the freedom to do a variety of things, both business and personal?

What would happen if I achieve my "success" in five years instead of three if I'm having fun throughout?

Procrastination is one thing. Conscious focus on incorporating all aspects into my life is another.

I want the balance. I want the variety. It is part of growing my business, only not in the terms of net profit of direct dollars.

When I look at success with my definition and not the voices of what I think society expects:

- I feel privileged
- I know I will get what I want
- My stress level goes down

And I know it's not only not so bad, it's pretty darn great!

To Strip or Not to Strip

I was asked if I would volunteer at a fundraising event. My role, with several other's, was selling raffle tickets in skimpy holiday attire, consisting only of boxer shorts, boots, socks and a Santa hat! In addition, at the end of the evening, we would be available for photo opportunities with the guests.

While I was flattered to be asked, the thought of doing this terrified me. It brought up my insecurities and fears.

I realized I had two choices.

I could decline the offer and not experience my insecurities and fears. Or I could confront them.

I'm a coach. So I chose the second option.

Prior to the event, I thought about what was true and what my mind told me. I talked to a few people about it. I find verbalizing insecurities and fears takes away a lot of their power.

By the time I got to the event, I was able to be in the moment. I ended up having a lot of fun and helped raise money for a worthy cause.

By confronting my fears I was able to:

- Enjoy the moment
- Be my *true* self
- Open myself up to other possibilities in life

So while I'm not looking to become a professional stripper, the experience I had in confronting my fears is useful for me to remember so I become more *fearless* to make the most of my life.

Turning on the TV

It's not so simple to turn on the television anymore. Without some kind of service you will get static.

I remember when I decided to get more current and drop my VCR and go digital. Since I had AT&T high speed internet and long distance, it made sense to go with the Satellite Dish and DVR.

Little did I know how complex this process would be.

It started when the service guy came out and informed me they couldn't get a signal from my house.

So now I had to think of alternatives.

Comcast, our major cable company had several options, depending on whether or not I switch my internet as well.

I called AT&T, and I wasn't under contract anymore to stay with the internet I had with them, but they promptly lowered my monthly cost and gave me 13 phone features I really didn't need for only 36 cents more a month.

While it still cost a little more to have AT&T then Comcast for the internet, changing would mean a coordination of installing cable I wasn't interested in doing. So I thought I'd stay with AT&T for the internet and go with Comcast for the cable.

There was a big price difference between basic cable and standard cable, but they were having a three-month special for more channels than I knew existed plus a premium channel.

However, in order to have the DVR, I would need to keep the digital cable which was included in the three-month special and the cost of this would probably be the same as renting a two bedroom apartment somewhere in the Midwest.

It occurred to me that I was doing all this to make sure I didn't miss an episode of 24.

Then AT&T found a signal so I could stay with them.

So now I have 120 channels, of which I may watch five.

But I have the DVR!

I never had trouble taping to a VCR but it's so much easier with the DVR.

It almost makes the hassle with all the choices and alternatives worth it.

Actually the end result made it worth it.

There are a lot of times when there are numerous choices, all appearing overwhelming, and at the moment, not worth pursuing.

But, many times these choices are part of the process and are necessary to pursue to get the result.

When I'm overwhelmed and remember what I'm striving for:

- I can break whatever is overwhelming into smaller steps
- I can make decisions
- I know I will get my outcome

Now it's time to go high definition!

Unemployed and Double Parked

After I was laid-off from a job, I was busy doing errands. I couldn't find parking so I double parked to do one errand.

I ran into someone I knew and started talking. We started talking about the changes in our lives. I had to cut the conversation short because I didn't want to get a ticket. I told him "*I'm sorry I have to run. I'm unemployed and double parked!*"

We both laughed.

But it was more than that to me.

It was a fun way to look at a time in my life when I was both fearful and excited.

I had a realistic and good attitude.

When I continue to have a realistic and good attitude about changes in my life:

- I keep my sense of humor
- I am true to myself and to my feelings
- I'm open to the possibilities

We have choices to uses phrases such as *unemployed and double parked* in a scary, demeaning way or as a tool for encouragement.

What Are My Parking Issues?

I was meeting a fellow coach for lunch. She lives in the suburbs and was concerned about the parking situation. I told her it shouldn't be a problem, particularly for the time of day we were getting together. Throughout our email correspondence, she kept referring to the parking and putting out positive energy for it to be easy!

This made me laugh. Something I put no attention on was a major source of concern to someone else.

It also made me think. The woman I was meeting is a dynamic person and an excellent and successful coach. Yet, she has created a situation for herself, namely *the difficulty of parking in the city* to the point where she either tries to avoid the city or stresses when she comes to town.

Parking isn't my issue. True, it can be difficult on some days and in certain neighborhoods, but it's the way it is; I accept it as city life.

But where in my life am I making things difficult while others don't seem to consider it an issue?

What are my *parking issues*?

Why is it that things I _focus_ on too much can cause me to stress, procrastinate, or avoid, and the things I _do_ simply happen?

What if I applied the strategy of *simply* doing to the things I focus on too much?

When I apply the principles of _just doing_ to areas of my life where I focus too much:

- I keep it simple
- I feel more energized
- I get into action faster

I'm going to take on a new attitude. If I can find parking pretty easily in San Francisco, I can do anything! This will help alleviate issues which hold me back.

When our focus is "*I can do anything*" we drop our parking issues.

What Else Can I Buy at 10% Off?

I'm not sure how, but I had a 10% discount on everything I bought at one of our local supermarkets. This went on for a couple of months.

I happened to be at the store on the last day of the 10% off. I needed to pick up a few produce items. When I realized it was the last day of the discount I automatically went into mind spinning gear mode.

What else do I need to buy from the store? What will I need in the next six weeks, six months, and six years...anytime in the future that I can buy now with this 10% discount?

How much money can I spend now to save 10%?

Should I spend time walking up and down the aisles?

I took a breath instead.

Then had a good laugh at myself!

I was grateful for having this discount for a reason I couldn't remember and remembered what I did buy with the discount. This seemed a lot calmer than trying to figure out what else I could buy at the eleventh hour.

When I got grateful about having this rather than thinking about how much more I could get from it:

- My stress and anxiety levels were down
- My gratitude was up
- I was open to appreciation rather than a lack of anything

Now, if I could only figure out how I got that discount!

What We Do Matters

I attended a friend's birthday dinner celebration. He shared stories about how each person at the party had impacted his life.

One story he shared was when he was trying a new experience. He was going away for a weekend with a group of strangers. A friend of his was supposed to join him but cancelled at the last moment. My friend almost decided not to go but in the end, since it was paid for, went anyway.

As everyone was waiting for the carpool caravan to begin the journey, he was off to the side standing alone.

Someone walked up to him and said hello. This made him feel welcome, and the weekend became a highlight for him and changed his life forever. He became more involved with the organization which had put on this trip, eventually becoming the chairman.

This might not have happened if that someone hadn't gone up to him and say hello.

As it turns out, I was that "someone"

I don't remember this incident.

I don't doubt I went up and said hello, I just don't remember. It wasn't significant to me.

But what an impact it had on him.

What we each do, all the time, has impact on others. Whether intentional or subconsciously, we affect the people around us. It is a gift and power I take for granted, or truthfully don't think about too often.

When I do think about it and realize what I do has impact on others:

- I aim to do my best
- Each moment becomes a conscious point in time
- I am more alive because what I do matters – and in ways I'll never know!

In this circumstance, my unconscious hello to someone ended up being a hello for life.

What's Your Strategy?

My tennis doubles partner and I were preparing for a match. We had a practice set with another doubles from our team.

They walloped us in the set even though we were pretty evenly matched, and we had beaten them in a competitive match some weeks before.

At the end of this set our coach asked us

What was your strategy?

What?

I thought we were only practicing.

Oh.

I guess, maybe, we should have had one anyway.

So my doubles partner and I had a brief conversation.

We won the next set.

Wow.

This simple question got us to have a brief conversation. I can't even remember the details of what we said. But, it obviously inspired a dialogue which helped us get focused.

I think I believed since we were *only practicing* we didn't have to have a strategy.

I think I also believed that it takes *work* to create a strategy. But in reality, it takes *more work* not to create one.

When I take time to create a strategy, whether I'm at work or play:

- I have a particular focus
- I tend to have more fun
- I am more involved

For me, having a strategy can make work more efficient and play more fun.

Good strategy.

Where It Could Lead

For a few years I've been giving workshops for an employee's assistance program. These workshops are on various topics such as *leadership, communications*, and *dealing with difficult people*. They can last anywhere from 30 minutes to two hours. Sometimes I do two or three in a day; sometimes only one.

I mentioned this work to a peer who said he wouldn't want to do something like this because it wasn't worth his time. His thinking was while the hourly pay was good and I get paid for travel expenses, I don't get paid for my travel time; therefore, the hourly wage is not worth it.

I have a different take on this. Doing the workshops energizes me, I meet new people, and I never know *where it could lead*.

One time I had two workshops with a three-hour gap in between. I have a good friend and former coworker who lived nearby, and we met for a late breakfast/early lunch.

As we were catching up, I mentioned my new additional business focus, which is going into the realm of public speaking. She thought for a moment and mentioned that she thought she could use me later in the year! It turns out that she sits on the board of an association that always needs good speakers; she has seen me in front of a room and knew I could deliver.

This gig turned out to be a reality!

If I hadn't done those other workshops, I'm not sure I ever would have mentioned my new business focus to my friend. While I do see her from time to time, who knows if our conversation would have taken this business turn. I was at the right place at the right time, and it wouldn't have occurred if I wasn't doing those other workshops.

When I'm locked to stringent parameters, that's all I'll see. When I'm open to *where it can lead*:

- I might do something which I enjoy doing well although at the moment may not look financially sound
- I embrace opportunities
- I see different ways to do the same thing

Where's the Maple Syrup?

I was on vacation and decided to have the French toast at the breakfast buffet - of course I wanted some maple syrup to put on the French toast.

I couldn't find the maple syrup. I asked someone where it was and was told that it was on the table with the other condiments.

I still couldn't find it.

Finally someone came over and showed me where it was.

It was right in front of me the whole time!

I was looking for a jar containing maple syrup. It was in a small plastic box, clearly marked maple syrup.

Because I had only one image in mind for the syrup, I didn't see it the way it was. This is all despite the evidence all around me.

All the different jellies, the ketchup – they were in small boxes, there were no jars!

I had a focus, a visual, and didn't see any other possibilities.

Where else in my life am I so focused I can't see other alternatives? Where else am I limiting myself to possibilities?

What I focus on is what I get – or don't get.

If I'm looking for maple syrup in a jar, I don't see maple syrup in a box.

If I'm looking for where something isn't going right in my life or business, I'm focusing on the limitations, not the achievements.

When I allow myself to see alternatives:

- I'm open to possibilities
- I allow my creativity and imagination to flow within me
- I'm not narrow minded

Who Will Come and See Me?

In my 20's and early 30's I would worry about who would take care of me or who would see me if something happened to me. I didn't worry about this incessantly, but I pondered this from time to time.

Then something happened to me.

I broke my leg.

I didn't have time to worry.

And, people showed up. It worked out.

Worry keeps me out of the present and in instead, makes me focus on fear and stress. It prevents me from getting what I want because I'm focused on what may or may not ever happen.

This past experience seems a great reminder to me in my present life.

When I go down the path of worry, I remember one of my ultimate worries and how, when the situation came to fruition, the reality of what happened was very different than the worry in my mind.

When I remember this:

- I am grounded
- I am serene
- I am confident

And I don't worry.

Winning Two Years in a Row—What Does It Really Mean?

My softball team won the division playoffs. We went to the World Series. We won for the second year in a row.

It seems somewhat surreal for me to be on a winning team. If I doubted my contribution to the team the first time, I certainly didn't the second. It showed me the first wasn't a fluke.

I started participating in sports later in my life. Back in my twenties if I made a list of goals I wanted to accomplish, playing softball, let alone winning in softball, wouldn't have been on the list. It wasn't in my consciousness.

Yet it happened in my life – I'm glad and proud of the accomplishments and what I've learned from playing softball.

I got involved with softball because of someone named Joe. He wanted to put together a team. Through this endeavor, Joe and I became very good friends.

Joe had faith in me in areas I never would have had confidence. He had me play left field – I thought he was crazy but he insisted. This has become my main position, although at this past World Series I played left and right center as well!

Whenever I feel a lack of faith and confidence within myself, I remember the faith and confidence Joe had in me. When I remember this:

- I am inspired
- I remember I am my only limitation
- I know if I can play left field, I can do anything!

My very good friend Joe lost his battle to cancer. I miss him very much. But what haven't been lost are the lessons he taught me.

All that winning two years in a row means is winning two years in a row.

What makes it important is what inspired me to go there in the first place.

You Should Be!

I am now a faculty member of a pretty well known and established company which does management, leadership, and communications workshops.

The process of getting accepted definitely required patience, as they have many applicants for different positions all over the world.

I got to teach my first workshop, which went very well, so now I've been assigned other dates for future workshops.

I am in the system.

I was talking to my representative at the corporation. As the company has been around for over 50 years, the procedures for submitting expenses and getting reimbursed are very detailed, and the conversations are professional.

Saying my joining the company would be a *win-win* is the most colloquial slang you would hear.

Or so I thought.

I was having a pleasant conversation with the person who assigns me future classes and told her I was excited about my affiliation with them. Her blunt response was

You should be!

Immediately I started to laugh.

She was in the moment and blurted it out!

She then laughed as well.

There probably was a more professional way to say what she did.

But there couldn't have been a more effective way. It was blunt and very real.

When we let go of having to sound or act in a certain way:

- We begin to be genuine
- We can react from our intuitions
- We become more effective

And we laugh more.

You're Going to Have to Make Do

I was meeting my workout partner at the gym at 8 a.m. one morning. I wanted to make the appointment a little bit later because it would flow better with my day. However, this was the time that worked best for him..

I got to the gym a few minutes late. He wasn't there. I waited a bit, and he still didn't come. I called him up, and he answered. He apologized and said he wasn't feeling well and wouldn't make it.

I was a little put out. Couldn't he have called me?

I started to think of how I could've gone to the gym later. I bumped into another friend and mentioned this to him. He said.

You're going to have to make do.

I smiled.

That's my line!

I often say this to my clients or my students in a class I'm teaching.

But, just because I coach and teach this, it doesn't necessarily mean I always remember it. I constantly need to be reminded that I can't control many things. Well, most things!

Sometimes timing works out; sometimes it doesn't.

Sometimes people are responsible the way you want them to be, sometimes they're not.

But when I heard my friend say, "You're going to have to make do," I let go of what could have been and looked at what was.

When I allow myself to accept, "You're going to have to make do:"

- I alleviate conflicts
- I make the most of a situation
- I experience things I wouldn't have if I didn't make do

I love my work because I'm always reminded by others what it is I continually need to do for my clients and for myself. And this happens anywhere, including when I bump into someone at the gym.

Bonus Stories

101 stories of shift sounded like a great number for the book. But as I was pulling together stories I had written and sent out, and others which I wrote but never showed anyone, and as I continually write new stories, I realized it would be appropriate to add more stories to show the power of shift is endless and ongoing.

Enjoy the extra stories!

1902

As most people reading this know, I scheduled April 1 for as many people to buy my book on Amazon as possible. Without knowing why, I was hoping to get into the top 100.

The day began.

I got some early e-mails from people saying they bought my book!

At 10 a.m. I decided to check my ranking – actually I didn't realize the ranking is right on the main page, but once I figured it out, I went to look.

I was ranked 19,200.

This boggled my mind. I thought it was a very high number!

Of course, I realized I had nothing to compare this to, since I never checked my ranking before. I remembered that my mother's book was on Amazon –about 10 years ago it was put on Amazon and there hadn't been much activity with the book for a while, so I thought I'd check to see her ranking.

It was ranked at almost 2 million!

After getting over the shock that there were that many books out there (and who knows how many more past 2 million the list of books goes!), I felt 19000 wasn't so bad.

I then decided to check a few other books.

A book on Muhammad Ali was ranked around 426,000.

Jane Fonda had a book from the mid 90s – it was ranked about 26,000.

I was ahead of two-time Academy award winner Jane Fonda! Pretty cool!

Since they update the rankings every hour, I looked to see my ranking at 11 a.m.

3029!

My ranking went up 16,000 in an hour!

The next hour it was down to 2117.

It went up and down throughout the day. At 10:45 p.m. it was ranked 1902, which I believe is the lowest it got.

If I had known the day before my ranking would get to only approximately 1900, when I wanted to be in the top 100, I would have been very disappointed.

As it was, I felt pretty good.

Why?

I figured about 10% of my mailing list would purchase the book (somewhere between 50 and 60 people). By the e-mail responses I got, I believe the percentage is higher.

With the exception of one or two *please unsubscribe me* e-mails, most responses I got were enthusiastic and encouraging.

What I heard would happen did happen. By getting people to purchase the book on the same day, it did go up in ranking.

What did I expect would happen if I got into the top 100?

I wasn't sure; I only wanted it. Well, maybe in the future.

I wouldn't be telling the truth if I didn't say I had a few moments of disappointment. But they were only a few.

There is opportunity in what I achieved even though I didn't get to the goal I wanted (a goal which was based on desire, not on realistic expectations).

When I recognize this opportunity:

- I can be proud of getting the first edition of my book out there in the world.
- I can be in awe by the number of people who supported me.
- I can use what happened as a stepping stone to what's next!

Oprah in 2010?! Okay how about 2012?

The Cost of Doing Business

I often do work for which I'm not paid. This includes preparation for training, paperwork for coaching, and writing.

In fact, much of my work doesn't include payment.

In all honesty, sometimes I get tired of doing this work for no payment.

I have expressed this at times. One friend summed it up and said:

Well, that's the cost of doing business.

He's correct.

When I look at it more closely, it really isn't about doing the work for no payment.

It's usually about not wanting to do the work at all!

Whether it's the type of work, or the timing of when it's happening, there are moments when I don't want to be doing what I'm doing.

If what I find disconcerting is the type of work, then I need to examine why I'm doing it and if it's worth it for my professional or personal growth.

If it's the timing of the work, is there something I can do about it?

We all have costs of doing business.

For me, as an entrepreneur, the cost of doing business can include many hours of prep for no money.

For those with full time jobs, it's commute time and costs or having to physically be somewhere for more hours then they may wish.

We all have costs.

When I acknowledge to myself everyone has costs to doing business:

- I remember the flexibility I have
- I reexamine tasks to make sure they are aligned with my goals
- I laugh when I blame management for any stress I have since I am management

The good news is whenever I ask my boss for time off, I always get it. I'm such a nice boss!

The Different Miracle

I decided to volunteer on Christmas morning to give out a meal to a senior who was alone and wouldn't be leaving home. Since I had two parties to go to later in the day, I thought this could be a good start to what the holiday season is supposed to mean.

When I got to the location to get the gift and food as well as the name and address of the person to whom I would be delivering it, things were slightly chaotic. They had different parts of the city listed where deliveries were needed. However, they had more volunteers than they had assignments.

A woman in front of me in line said *I guess we should let go of any expectations we have of volunteering today.*

I smiled and agreed.

I also wondered if I had any expectations.

I didn't think I did. *I only hoped I would visit a wise old soul who would tell me a story so compelling I felt like I was flashed back in time and experienced the lifetime lesson this person was telling me. The story would move me so and change the way I viewed life forever. When I would contact this person the next day, the number would be disconnected, and when I called the volunteer office, they would tell me this person never existed.*

I would have experienced a miracle, a Christmas miracle!

I guess I had expectations.

What really happened is this: When I arrived at the designated address to deliver the gift and food, the person I hoped to visit wasn't home. I ended up leaving everything with the security guard.

Just a slightly different scenario.

But I wasn't disappointed. I'm at a point in my life where I recognize that while I want things to happen a certain way (whether realistic or fantasy) it is often best to let expectations go and simply accept what is.

When I can take the reality of an outcome which wasn't what I planned:

- I can see what works and doesn't work
- I can look at viable alternatives for the future
- I can look at why I wanted a specific outcome which didn't happen

This leads to acceptance rather then conflict.

This is a miracle for every day of the year.

Having a Bad Arm

I was at a softball practice with a new team. One thing I
immediately noticed was that most of the outfielders could
throw the ball a lot farther then I could. I usually liked a
cutoff (either second baseman or short stop) to come out a
little to the outfield so I could throw the ball to him. A lot of
the others didn't need this – they could throw the ball right to
second or third base.

We had a guest coach come to one of our practices. Sometime
during the practice, he was giving strategy. He told the infield
to figure out which of the outfielders had bad arms, so they
knew when to go out to intercept the ball.

I immediately spoke up and said

*I don't have a bad arm; I just can't throw the ball as far as the
others.*

This remark went completely over his head.

But it's true – I don't have a bad arm. Its fine, in fact it's in
great shape. I just haven't learned how to throw a ball farther
then I do.

Maybe I never will. At this point, I probably don't really care
to – but it's different to say I have a bad arm versus I don't
throw the ball as far as others.

The former implies there is nothing I could do about it. The
latter allows for a change to occur.

Saying *I have a bad arm* is de-motivating and could be
demeaning. *I have a bad arm* could be a metaphor for any
trite and thoughtless response given to you by a friend, peer,
mentor, or boss.

The intent doesn't have to be harmful, and yes, the recipient
can be a little sensitive.

Nonetheless, if not thought through, it can be damaging.

Thinking I have a bad arm could dissuade me from continuing to play or could make me play worse because I'm focused on a negative.

But when I interpret what is said in a way which is acceptable to me:

- I still can be motivated
- I can figure out alternatives if I wish
- I can still be confident

I own the fact that I don't throw the ball far. Maybe that's why I enjoy tennis more!

Holding In My Gut

I used to hold my gut in and feel I had to keep it a secret because I thought it was vain. I resigned myself to this superficiality as an attempt to keep a six pack, okay maybe a three pack stomach.

In what I thought was unrelated, I also noticed my lower back had more frequent pains. It got to the point where I would notice it every time I would bend over. It didn't surprise me, considering things happen with age, and my involvement with sports was increasing, rather than decreasing.

I mention my lower back pain to my massage therapist. He told me to hold in my stomach when I bent down. Holding in the gut reinforces the back.

Amazingly, I found this to be true.

When I hold my gut in and bend down my lower back doesn't hurt.

So now I'm holding in my stomach all the time. I want it to get so routine that it's an unconscious movement.

So the same action which caused me embarrassment now causes me to feel physically better.

A lot better.

The same exact action.

Not different results – while I thought I was holding my stomach in to maintain the best physical shape I could muster, I was also helping my back. I only didn't know it at the time.

The difference was the reasons I was doing the action.

And those reasons, for me, were the difference between a legitimate and superficial reason to do the action.

Other people may not have this issue for this particular action.

But we all have actions, which we feel great doing or are embarrassed doing

But what if those embarrassing actions are actually good for us?

If we are open to this possibility:

- We can see progress where we once saw discomfort.
- Something unexpectedly great can happen.
- We might take more chances.

There are always actions we do which don't serve us. But there are many which might if we're open to the possibility.

In this case, my lower back is very grateful.

How on Earth Did I Get This Speaking Gig?

I wanted to do more speaking gigs to get out there to practice my craft and generate more business. Someone told me about a group I hadn't heard of, but I went to their website and contacted someone there.

A woman called me back and told me their group was different than others in that it was a little older and more conservative. She asked my topic and said it could be something the group loved or rejected depending on my content and delivery.

After talking with her we agreed on a date on which I'd speak. At the end of our talk, she casually mentioned a place for me to see past speakers.

After the call and confirmed date, I went to see some of the confirmed speakers.

CEO of Bechtel Corporation
Former San Francisco mayor Frank Jordan
Then Supervisor now current mayor Gavin Newsom
Film Critic Jan Wahl
Trial Lawyers
Judges

And now Howard Miller.

What's wrong with this picture?

I got a little concerned.

I felt a little anxiety.

Actually I freaked out.

How was I every going to pull this off?

I did see the irony in my topic being *shifting difficult situations to positive opportunities* but nonetheless the anxiety and fear either grew or remained the same.

A couple of weeks before I was scheduled to speak, I happened to go back to the website to see someone else, someone from the State Assembly was speaking when I was supposed to speak.

I know I should have been agitated or angry I was replaced and no one told me.

But truthfully I was relieved.

I was prepared to put this down to fate.

My brother told me I need to contact them and get an explanation.

Damn.

I contacted them.

The woman had goofed.

I was given another date.

Then, things shifted.

First I noticed a member in the organization who I already knew. I contacted her – turns out she was inviting a guest who was a client of mine! Also, she was going to be the one to introduce me.

I started to look at this talk from what value it could give.

I was still a little anxious.

But the talk went off without a hitch.

Actually it was great!

All my fears were unfounded. All the time I spent worrying about it proved in vain (of course when does worrying ever help?!)

I went through whatever it was I went through.

But a shift happened when:

- I admitted my anxiety and fear to others
- I sought out familiarity in a situation which looked different
- I took the focus off my nervousness and looked at what purpose I was serving when speaking

I am now grateful for this speaking gig. It serves as a reminder to me of how my fears can limit me and how anything is possible when I get out of the fears.

It's An Honor to Be Nominated

How many times do we hear that from Hollywood celebrities? Indeed it is an honor, but don't they want to win, especially if they get nominated over and over again?

Towards the end of my first year playing tennis, the organization which runs most of the games I played in had its end of year banquet. Prior to the banquet they have nominations for several awards.

My manager blind copied me on an email in which he nominated me for Most Improved Player of the Year.

I was very humbled by the gesture. I certainly, along with several others, improved a lot. More importantly, I was passionate about playing and enjoyed the game and the process of improving.

Then, I found out they collected all the suggested nominees and created a ballot. This ballot of nominations would go out to the membership at large. The winners would be announced at the banquet.

This is tennis, not the Oscars. Yes, we're in California, but San Francisco not Hollywood!

So be it, the nominations were out and yes I was nominated.

My doubles partner (and good friend) was also nominated in my category.

But wait, he was also nominated for Rookie of the Year.

Why did he get two nominations and I only got one? And wait another player from my team, who started at the same time was also nominated for Rookie of the Year. Why wasn't I nominated for Rookie of the Year?

Then I laughed.

What was I thinking? What is the big deal? Was this really important to me?

I believe at one point in my life it would have been. I believe if it still were, I'd be honest about it, or at least not write about it to avoid having to think about it.

But the reality is I'm very proud at how much I've improved. I'm proud at how all of us improved. I know that I am more connected to the game and how much more I can be – this award doesn't add to or take away from this truth.

But what if one of the others wins and I don't?

It still doesn't take away how much I improved.

When I know this for myself:

- I am seeing the forest from the trees.
- I enjoy the process of what I'm doing.
- I'm focused on what matters to me.

And the Most Improved Player was...

Inspired by Tony Randall

Without a doubt, *The Odd Couple* is one of the funniest television shows I've ever seen. I've watched most episodes many times and still laugh as if it's my first time seeing the program. The chemistry between Jack Klugman and Tony Randall is sublime, and *Felix Unger* is one of the funniest, most outrageous and over-the-top characters I have ever enjoyed, played to perfection by Tony Randall, who died at the age of 84.

Tony Randall, his character and the show, have brought immeasurable joy to my life. My humor, which has sustained me during high and low points throughout the years, was molded from Felix Unger. For my brother and me, the wit of *The Odd Couple* created a bond and language which still exists today.

Simply put, Tony Randall inspired me in my life.

I find myself wondering who else inspires me, and who do I inspire. It's certainly harder for me to know and to list who I inspire. But because I know there are many people who inspire me, it's vital that I believe (and I do!) that I inspire people as well.

To know I inspire others gives me:

- More confidence in myself
- A feeling of connection to other people
- The desire to do more to bring out the best in me

I think its time to watch an *Odd Couple* rerun!

Knowing Barbara DeVries

Someone I had met at a networking event invited me to a cocktail party. While I was there, I started talking to someone who was new to the healthcare industry. He started telling me the type of work he did and then he said, *I know Barbara DeVries.*

Where on earth did this come from? I'm not in the healthcare industry, so why would I know someone unless they were famous for some vaccine or had made the news? His statement was a non sequitur.

What was really strange is that I do indeed know Barbara DeVries! We had met about 15 years ago, became good friends, and then lost touch. His mentioning her name made me think of her again, and I reconnected with Barbara last year.

We are friends again. In addition, I've done some consulting work for her company! Not only does knowing Barbara once again enhance my personal life, but my business has benefited as well!

I love this story and reminding myself of it because when I do it gives me:

- Faith and hope that everything works out
- Confidence to move forward
- The excitement and wonder that you never know what opportunities are out there and what can happen by talking to even one person!

So if something isn't working out as planned, maybe in the long run, it is!

The Last Row of the Plane

I was returning from my New York vacation. On the return flight I was assigned seat 34D, which, as it turns out, was in the last row of the plane. As I sat down I got a little sad as I remembered when I use to fly more often and was in the front section of the plane. In just a few years, I went from a steady paycheck and the frequent flier section of the plane, to the up and down income generated from my (growing!) business and to the last row of the plane!

However, instead of going deeper into negative thoughts, I practiced what I preach to my clients and let these thoughts go. What is to be is to be, and I should see the opportunity instead of the negativity.

As it turned out, after the plane filled up, I had all three seats to myself. I was able to stretch out and enjoy my music, read a book and write in my journal, with lots of room and privacy. I was able to reflect back on the great week I had in Manhattan with my parents and friends, the unexpected trip to my cousins at their beautiful house on the lake, and all the Broadway shows I had seen.

When the plane landed, I had at least five extra minutes on the plane than most people. During that time I was able to check my messages, use the facilities located at the rear of the plane, so that when I got off the plane I walked right from the plane to the sky train to the BART station (which showed up in less than five minutes).

By being present to the opportunities of the moment and not focusing on what I thought could be better I was able to:

- Stay focused on what was going on
- Be the most energetic and alive I could be at that moment
- Appreciate how much is always being offered to me if I am willing to see it!

So when something is not going my way, I hope I can remember to ask myself *what is going right?* I'll see how much is going my way!

Like Giving Sugar to a Baby

My brother told me awhile back when my eldest niece was celebrating her first Halloween that they took her around trick-or-treating. To keep her aware and awake they allowed her to eat something with sugar. They could see the immediate effect the sugar had on her and then could see the crash. They could then give her a little more and start the cycle over.

Fortunately, they didn't do this for long that night and, as far as I know didn't repeat this in future events!

I was at a retreat with lots of people. I noticed at different times during the weekend I was connecting or not connecting with others.

It all depended on my thought process.

If I was having negative thoughts, I could go deeper into the thoughts. Once I realized what I was doing I could stop it, say something different to myself, and then start smiling and getting along with others.

Like giving sugar to a baby, I could change my mood and attitude quickly.

But I'm an adult.

How often do I go to pity poor me or selfish thoughts? I'm not beating myself for having them; it can be human to have them.

Yet it could also be habitual.

It takes a small effort to *shift* these thoughts.

When I do shift my negative thoughts to ones which help me connect more with others and myself:

- I get out of the mood I was in
- Things can happen differently
- I really am having so much more fun!

And I don't have to eat sugar to do this!

The Middle Seat on a Plane

I was flying to the east coast. I got up very early for a 7AM flight.

I had booked the flight at least a month before and received an aisle seat.

I like aisle seats because they're more open and less claustrophobic.

When I got to my seat there was someone already in the window seat.

As the plane was about to depart a mother and son got on. She was panicked. There weren't seats for both of them to sit together.

There were two middle seats. One in the row in front of me and one next to me.

This panicked mother sat next to me and was complaining about having to be separated from her son.

She was, in my opinion, being pretty indignant, trying to demand from the flight attendant that seats get switched.

She asked the woman sitting in the window seat if she would switch with her son. The woman said no.

For some reason she didn't ask me.

Maybe she knew what I'd say.

First of all, it appeared that her son, who was about 8 years old and already playing with his video games, was not panicked.

She was.

And who's going to want to switch a window or aisle seat for a middle seat?

I think, to me, what was most disturbing and annoying was that this woman was blaming everyone around her for the situation.

She didn't take responsibility – maybe if she had tried explaining in a less panicked and abrasive manner someone would have switched with her.

Maybe I would have switched seats.

No, who am I kidding; I wouldn't have given up my aisle seat for a middle seat!

Eventually, the young woman sitting next to her son gave the mother her seat. I think she realized she wouldn't get any rest and figured the middle seat was the lesser of two evils.

The mother thanked her although her thanks seemed a little insincere since it seems she thought she should have had the seat all along.

It's difficult enough when a friend or family member tries to lay guilt on you. It's difficult and awkward in a different way when it's done by a stranger.

I'm not against parents and children sitting together. I can empathize and understand why the mother would want to switch seats.

But coming from an entitled expectation rubs me the wrong way.

When we can come from ownership and responsibility when requesting something from others:

- We may not get what we want, but if we do, it'll be from a desire to help, not guilt
- We might see other alternatives to our requests

- Someone else might come up with an idea which satisfies everyone

The flight attendants did offer free drinks and food to the woman who moved next to me.

This is probably not the first time they have had to deal with this kind of difficult situation.

My Algae Eater Stopped Cleaning the Fish Tank!

I have a 20 gallon fish tank filled with tropical fish. I always loved my algae eater. It would clean everything, all the time. He (I decided to give a pronoun to my algae eater) would either be on the bottom of the tank getting rid of the waste from the other fish, on the sides furiously scraping away to keep them spotless, cleaning the live plants, or on occasion, and what I think was his personal favorite, eating the remains of a dead fish I didn't find in time.

I always wanted him to expand from the tank and clean my house. Wouldn't it be wonderful to see this fish in various parts of my home scrubbing away and keeping it clean?

Nonetheless, he grew in proportion to the tank, and I've been fortunate to see a small fish transform to a pretty large impressive looking fish.

He is also my oldest fish, about 10 years old.

All in all I've been very happy with him.

Until he stopped cleaning the tank.

I can't put an exact date on this. I think I first noticed the tank being dirty. Okay, I still clean it every four to six weeks. So, it was probably due for cleaning. But after I cleaned the tank, I noticed a day or two later that it was pretty dirty again. Maybe I didn't do a thorough cleaning, so I cleaned certain parts again. But it got dirty very quickly.

This is when I noticed – the algae eater was just sitting there.

At first I thought he was dead, and I was a little sad.

But then I noticed him breathing, and he would move every so often. But instead of cleaning, he was hanging out, lying around different parts of the tank.

Now I'm not happy with him.

I suppose he's had enough. He's had his share of being around the tank. He's seen it all. He's grown as large as he desires.

He's content.

Can I blame him?

Maybe I'm envious. How often do I continue to do something even when I've had enough? How often do I do things out of routine, because I'm in a rut, because I can't bother changing, or I have fear of change?

My fish knew when it was time to stop. It seems to be quite happy living the new life. No guilt, no agonizing about the decision.

When I stop something, whether it's a job or something I've done for years, or something which keeps playing over and over in my mind:

- I allow myself to feel the uncertainty of change.
- I open myself up to something new.
- I'm content – for the moment.

I believe I need to get another algae eater for my tank. Of course, I'll make sure this won't affect the longevity of my retired algae eater.

But I'm content my 10 year old fish won't be cleaning any more.

My Mother the Coach

I was on a work assignment near where my parents live. I wanted to improve some tennis skills while I was there.

My mother has played tennis for most of her adult life. She has been in numerous tournaments and is fairly competitive. While she still plays, she has limited her play time due to various ailments.

But that didn't mean she couldn't be on the court and share some pointers to break my bad habits.

I asked her, and she agreed to spend some time helping me.

When we first got on the court, I was resistant. After all, she is my mother, the person who can push my buttons more quickly and faster than most other people on this planet. She can even do this without my talking to her, the mother –son triggers are internal and can happen unconsciously!

As we proceeded, I was aware of her talking.

But, I wasn't listening.

I was analyzing and judging everything she said. Overall, what I was doing was censoring everything ending with the same thought:

Mom, be quiet already.

Then I realized what I was doing.

I wasn't listening at all. I was tuning her out because I thought she was nagging me.

But, I had asked to share some pointers with me.

She was offering her expertise.

I realized this and started listening.

What she said made sense – not all of it, but I don't think one connects with everything any instructor says.

But what connected with me helped as I continued to practice. My backhand and serve started to improve.

Because I started listening.

To my mother.

The lesson here isn't to always listen to your mother.

Taking it to a more global level, where do I stop listening because of a judgment I have?

When I start listening where I wasn't listening before:

- I learn
- I can improve
- I can take what works and leave the rest, but usually I take something

And I'm certain if I can make this change with Mom, I can do it with anyone.

Our Town

I was in New York and looking forward to seeing several shows. I pre-purchased tickets to some shows; others I would get on the half price line.

I was meeting a friend to see one show. It is sometimes challenging to see something with him as he lives in New York, works in the industry, so he has seen most shows by the time I get to town.

To my surprise he hadn't seen the revival of *Hair*. It was up for half price.

He debated whether he wanted to go since chances were he could probably get complimentary house seats in the near future.

For some reason, the fact that I had never seen any production of *Our Town* came up in our conversation.

He was stunned I had never seen it. There was a production Off-Broadway. He had already seen it but wanted me to see it and would go again.

I really wanted to see *Hair*. I like the music.

But I went along with my friend's excitement and purchased tickets to the Off-Broadway production of *Our Town*.

Our Town is three acts.

During the first act, I was singing songs from *Hair* in my head.

During the second act, I connected with several of the themes and some of the lines.

During the third act, I had one of the most subtle and powerful experiences I have ever had in the theater.

What happened in the play connected with where I am in my life today and unexpectedly grabbed every part of me. I believe at one point I held my breath as I was listening and taking in what was going on in the play.

It was if there was a reason I had never seen any production of *Our Town* until then.

And to think I didn't want to go see the play!

I'm glad I wasn't willful and for some reason went with my friend's excitement. I would have missed out on this experience.

When I can let go (and there are times I can't!) of what I think I want and go with someone else's excitement:

- I allow myself to have an adventure
- I let go of my control
- I take risks

By going with my friend's excitement and seeing *Our Town* and not *Hair*, I still

Let the sun shine in!

The Perfection of Mediocrity

A friend and I went to see a one man show. While the topic was intriguing the execution was mediocre at best. (Note to all: *I am purposely not saying what the show was about to give you an idea of the feelings of dissatisfaction we had when the show ended. I'm trying to have you experience what I felt, without hopefully, making this reading mediocre!*)

After the show, we started talking about where the show felt flat and what we might do differently.

It was a rather short one man show, which in this case was merciful. But since it was early, we decided to go back to the theater to see if the actor was still there to see if he wanted to hear our ideas. Unfortunately, he had already left.

We continued to talk about the show's premise and the possible ways to have gone with the show.

After about 45 minutes I looked at my friend and said: *Do you realize all we've talked about is this mediocre show. Would we have talked about it for so long if we had loved the show?*

We both laughed but also acknowledged how the show being so-so was something we both needed this particular evening.

Having the show fall short gave us a chance to use our own creative process. It helped us appreciate the work it takes to make a show good. When something is excellent sometimes the process appears seamless.

When I can be challenged by something which falls short:

- I truly can shift perspective to something which motivates
- I have a chance of being nicer to myself when I fall short
- I understand a little bit more that what we do matters

It was probably 10 years into her career when I saw the true genius of Meryl Streep. While I always thought she was a great actress, seeing *The Bridges of Madison County* catapulted her in my mind to the best. This is because I thought this movie was a monumental tower of boredom.

Yet she shined.

I thought if she could shine in such mediocrity what a treat to see her in quality work.

This recent one man show reminded me of this perfection of mediocrity.

The Quality of Life

I saw a well written and brilliantly acted (including Laurie Metcalf and JoBeth Williams) play about loss, illness ,and life titled *The Quality of Life.*

The following morning I was on a teleconference where the topic was *The How of Happiness.*

While on this teleconference, I got an email informing me that one of the guys on my tennis team had committed suicide.

Besides the bizarre timing of all these incidents, the suicide left me pretty shocked.

I wasn't close friends with this guy, but I did practice with him several times, and had shared a few meals and conversations. He was a doctor and seemed like everyone else. He was a little quiet, but most people are quiet compared to me.

Some say suicide is selfish and extremely hard for the loved ones left behind. I can't imagine what his family was going through and can't begin to understand any anger, guilt or other emotions they felt.

But if everything happens for a reason, what this disturbing and shocking news did for me was really to stop me in my tracks and get immediately grateful for my life.

For the moment I found out, all those negative thoughts I was having (ranging from work stress to politics to errands I had to do, etc.) stopped.

I focused on what I do have in my life and how, even when life has been low for me, I haven't gone to such an extreme answer to get rid of any pain.

When I can find something decent in something horrible that has happened:

- It gives me hope.
- I feel humbled.
- It shows me the power of life.

I don't think my tennis friend's death is worth this lesson, but it shows a ray of sun amidst a dark cloud.

Robert Wagner Was in Gone with the Wind

At least that's what my mother has been saying for a few years.

She was watching the movie on the Turner Classic Movie channel (TCM), and heard Robert Osborne announce before the movie to try and notice an un-credited 14-year-old Robert Wagner.

She didn't notice Robert Wagner, and no one she talked to seems to know he was in the movie.

I researched this online and couldn't find anything either. In fact, I found evidence to the contrary. Robert Wagner would not have been 14 when *Gone with the Wind* came out; he would have been younger.

His website and websites which talk about him never mentioned his being in this movie.

Still my mother insisted she heard it.

Recently, TCM reran *Gone with the Wind*. My mom watched to verify what she heard.

She didn't hear it. She now acknowledges she must've been mistaken in what he said.

This whole journey to this acceptance took about three years.

It got me thinking: haven't I, at times, thought I heard something which was never said?

Haven't I gotten myself into uncomfortable situations based on assumptions which weren't really true?

Quite a bit actually!

And, not only were these times frustrating for me ,they led to conflicts with others.

These frustrations and conflicts still occur for me.

But when I'm in conflict and can come to acceptance that my assumptions may not be true:

- The time frame of conflict shortens
- I can hear what really is being said
- I can still keep my opinion and respect others for theirs

So Robert Wagner wasn't in *Gone with the Wind*, but the original Superman was!

The Seven Is in the Right Place

When I was growing up in the 1970s, my dad was a math teacher. There was one time when I was in the room with him and he was grading quizzes. He uttered an exasperated sigh. I asked him what was wrong. He showed me.

He taught junior high students. One of the quiz questions was:

In 1975, the seven is in the ____ place.

The answer, of course, is the tens place.

The student wrote down the right place.

While my father sighed, I laughed. I thought it was creative and tried to convince my father to grade it with an open mind.

He marked it incorrect.

Years later, I was doing my yearly stint with Blue Cross Blue Shield teaching call center students. One of my students, who was quite bright and doing well, looked at me earnestly one day and asked:

What's the difference between Blue Cross and the Red Cross?

Well, this left me speechless. I mean, what's similar between them?

I don't really think I answered the question and left the situation a little dumbfounded.

But I realized later that cultural and generational differences can make comments sound absurd to some and inquisitive to others.

If we all thought the same way, how would we come up with something new or creative?

When I recognize that our differences can give us all different conclusions:

I am open to things I might consider absurd or stupid
I am (a little) more patient
I get some great stories to tell!

I'll never forget the math story which happened over 30 years ago. If it weren't for the thought process of a young student going awry due to creativity or not getting what was being taught, I wouldn't have the story.

For that, I'll mark him correct; the seven was in the right place.

The Show Must Go On

I've always recommended that my fellow instructors take an improvisation class at least once in their lives. Besides being fun, it's a great way to experience how to make things up when something doesn't go the way you plan.

As an instructor, I can guarantee that things won't go as planned.

Over the years, I have learned to be ready to make something from nothing.

I have had to teach software classes without the software.

I have had to teach with the students using the software while the developer was on the phone correcting it as they were using it.

I have had to teach workshops where the materials never showed up.

I have had to teach where half the class was missing because everyone had different directions on where the class was being held.

I have gone to teach a topic only to find out I was supposed to teach a completely different topic.

I had to continue teaching after someone in the front row passed out and had to be taken to the emergency room.

But, as they say, the show must go on.

Not to tempt fate, but I don't think anything could happen which I couldn't handle.

I recently taught a management course. It was one of those rare classes where I actually used the DVD supplied in class. The topic was *delegation.*

When I inserted the DVD, it didn't work.

Ok, I should have checked it out before class started that day.

I was perplexed as to why it didn't work when it had in the past, then I remembered before we had used a VHS tape, not a DVD.

I needed IT's help.

Everyone, take a 10 minute break!

Turns out this "DVD" only played on the computer, not the DVD player (not sure why).

So, we started watching the program.

Part of the way into the movie it started to stall. Got stuck, then moved on.

After it did this twice I thought it was unproductive to watch anymore so I shut it off.

Well now what do we do?

There was an exercise in the manual which I hadn't done in the past. I thought it was overkill and too detailed. But, since there was time I had everyone do the exercise.

It was a powerful and effective exercise which emphasized how to put delegation into action in a manner far better than any discussion or movie could have done.

I never would have known this if we hadn't had technical problems with the DVD.

When I remember something good could happen from a glitch, problem, or annoyance:

- I don't freak out over the problem
- I can see alternatives
- I look for opportunity

This exercise will now be a permanent part of this future workshop. That is, until something else which is unexpected happens and shows me yet another way.

Softball, Skipping and Dancing

One Monday morning I was exhausted when I woke up and wasn't motivated to get to work. I felt I hadn't relaxed during the weekend and was starting to go down the path of not having enough time which would make me feel overwhelmed.

I then remembered my day before and what I chose to do.

The day started with a softball game in the morning. From there I went to a special Skipping event a friend of mine was putting on (yes, you heard me, correctly, skipping!)

After skipping with everyone, I drove home to shower, eat, and head out dancing.

Any guesses why I was exhausted the next day?

What fulfilling reasons to be tired!

I had gotten to be outside, playing sports, mingling with all sorts of people and ended up dancing.

How lucky I am to be physically able to do all of those things and also have the time to make them an entire day's events.

When I look at those activities in this light on Monday morning:

- I am suddenly energized to get on with my day
- The physical activity from the day before invigorates the work for today
- I am relaxed

There is always value in what we do, even if it seems a waste of time. If anything, there are lessons to learn about what we don't want to do again.

When we have this attitude we can always be playing softball, skipping and dancing!

Welcome Home

At one point in my life, I traveled a lot for business. All told, the time totals about 7 years of business travel. As I told a friend during that time *I was in airports more than you thought about them.*

I remember always expecting, or rather wanting, my parents to be greeting me wherever I landed, no matter what time or where in the country I was landing.

It never happened of course.

I recently was traveling on vacation to Florida to visit my parents and play tennis.

My parents were picking me up at the Fort Lauderdale airport.

I couldn't remember the last time they had met me at the airport. I unconsciously believed those days were over.

Throughout the long journey, which included getting up at 3:30AM to make a 6AM flight, I was in a state of gratitude for this simple act.

How lucky to be my age and have two parents who are healthy enough to drive and get me.

Okay, so mom couldn't exactly remember how to get back to the car from baggage claim. But, that simply provided a good laugh.

For me to be able to see the gift of being greeted at the airport, to enjoy this state of the gratitude, is the antithesis of conflict. It is opportunity.

When I can be grateful for something others do for me:

- It helps me focus on opportunity instead of negatives
- I don't take for granted something I wish I had cherished

- I'm a little more inspired to do more for others as well

And when my parents picked me up from the airport it made me feel like I was home even though I was on the other side of the country.

Conclusion

When people find out I deal with conflict resolution and teach others how to deal with difficult people (with individuals and teams), they hope I can give them the solution, the ultimate answer to how to avoid and resolve conflicts with the difficult people in their lives.

If only I could guarantee them an outcome they want!

But since we are human beings, there is no mathematical formula or guaranteed quick solution to resolve anyone's conflict.

There are tools one can use, and I do guarantee if you use the tools, something will change. It may not be the outcome you desire, but you will receive change!

There are many different tools. No single tool works for everyone, and one isn't better than another.

One such tool is the gift of story.

The stories in this book, involving me or my clients, showed situations where a shift and change occurred. While you may not have related to every story, I hope there were some which reminded you of something in your life. May it have inspired you to possibly do something different in the future when you encounter a similar situation again.

I am truly humbled by the number of people who have thanked me for my stories and how they have related to them. There is always someone who values one story, while someone else really appreciates another. To me, this shows the power of story, the great differences between all of us, and how we can use these differences for discussion and disagreement while still maintaining a respect, so opportunity is created.

General Themes of the Stories of Shift

Acceptance
Acknowledgment
Appreciation
Being open to others
Being present
Centered and grounded
Confidence
Connection
Control
Daring
Energy
Excitement
Expectations
Faith
Fears: alleviate fears, confronting fears
Feeling love
Focus
Follow through
Get something done
Gifts
Giving
Gratitude
Hope
Humility
Inspiring others
Joy
Optimism
Overwhelm
Owning my time
Peace
Possibilities
Slower pace
Taking care of yourself
Time
Trust
Willingness

Howard Miller

Howard Miller is an executive and business coach, trainer, and facilitator. He is available for keynote talks, one on one & group coaching, meeting facilitation, and conducting team building, communication/behavioral skills workshops and assessments.

For further information, contact him at howard@fulcrumpointpartners.com.

www.ingramcontent.com/pod-product-compliance
Lightning Source LLC
LaVergne TN
LVHW011222080426
835509LV00005B/265